Bite into 98 Paula Deen's Baking Delights

Golden Fry Delights

Copyright © 2023 Golden Fry Delights
All rights reserved.

Contents

INTRODUCTION 7

1. Red Velvet Cake...9
2. Pecan Pie..10
3. Banana Pudding 11
4. Peach Cobbler 12
5. Key Lime Pie 13
6. Buttermilk Biscuits 14
7. Sweet Potato Pie 15
8. Chocolate Chess Pie 16
9. Coconut Cake..17
10. Apple Dumplings 18
11. Cornbread 19
12. Strawberry Shortcake 20
13. Caramel Cake 21
14. Lemon Bars 22
15. Southern Pecan Pralines 23
16. Blueberry Cobbler 24
17. Pound Cake 25
18. Mississippi Mud Pie 26
19. Sausage Gravy and Biscuits..27
20. Buttermilk Fried Chicken 28
21. Peach Upside-Down Cake 28
22. Sweet Tea...30
23. Chess Squares 30
24. Blackberry Cobbler 31
25. Buttermilk Pancakes...32
26. Hummingbird Cake..33
27. Fried Green Tomatoes 34

28. Bread Pudding..35

29. Southern Cornbread Dressing...36

30. Sweet Potato Casserole..37

31. Apple Pie 38

32. Butter Pecan Ice Cream..39

33. Baked Macaroni and Cheese..40

34. Gooey Butter Cake..41

35. Fried Chicken and Waffles...42

36. Cheese Straws 43

37. Strawberry Rhubarb Pie 44

38. Old-Fashioned Chocolate Layer Cake 45

39. Chicken and Dumplings..46

40. Lemon Meringue Pie...47

41. Coca-Cola Cake 48

42. Buttermilk Fried Shrimp 49

43. Peach Ice Cream..50

44. Biscuit Cinnamon Rolls 51

45. Sweet Potato Biscuits..51

46. Lemon Poppy Seed Bread..52

47. Hush Puppies..53

48. Southern Banana Bread...54

49. Apple Fritters 55

50. Cinnamon Sugar Donuts...57

51. Strawberry Jam Thumbprint Cookies 58

52. Coconut Cream Pie 59

53. Praline Pecan Bread Pudding 60

54. Brown Sugar Pecan Cookies..61

56. Southern Cornbread Pudding..62

57. Pimento Cheese Dip 63

58. Chocolate Pecan Pie Bars 64
59. Peach Pound Cake 65
60. Fried Okra 66
61. Blackberry Jam Cake 67
62. Sausage and Grits Casserole 68
63. Caramel Apple Upside-Down Cake 69
64. Bourbon Bread Pudding 70
65. Apple Cider Doughnuts 71
66. Sweet Potato Cinnamon Rolls 72
67. Peanut Butter Pie 73
68. Bacon Cheddar Cornbread 74
69. Lemon Blueberry Bundt Cake 75
70. Mississippi Mud Brownies 76
71. Baked Collard Greens 77
72. Southern-Style Banana Pudding Cheesecake 78
73. Buttermilk Fried Pork Chops 79
74. Pecan Sandies 80
75. Pumpkin Bread 81
76. Honey Butter Biscuits 82
77. Southern Peach Tea 83
78. Chocolate Fudge Cake 84
79. Buttermilk Panna Cotta 85
80. Sweet Potato Pancakes 86
81. Strawberry Swirl Pound Cake 87
82. Southern-Style Grits 88
83. Chocolate Chip Pecan Cookies 89
84. Lemon Icebox Pie 90
85. Cornbread Muffins 91
86. Bourbon Pecan Tart 92

87. Fried Catfish 93

88. Peanut Butter Fudge 94

89. Sweet Potato Waffles 95

90. Bourbon Balls 96

91. S'mores Pie 97

92. Shrimp and Grits 98

93. Cherry Cobbler 99

94. Caramel Apple Bread 100

95. Buttermilk Ranch Biscuits 101

96. Bourbon-Soaked Cherry Cake 102

97. Southern Fried Apples 103

98. Mississippi Mud Cookies 104

CONCLUSION 106

INTRODUCTION

Welcome to the sweet and savory world of Southern baking! In this delectable cookbook, titled "Bite into the South: 98 Paula Deen's Baking Delights," we embark on a culinary journey through the rich and diverse flavors of the South, guided by the renowned celebrity chef, Paula Deen. From mouthwatering pies and decadent cakes to irresistible cookies and indulgent bread, this collection of recipes is a treasure trove of Southern baking delights.

Paula Deen has long been celebrated for her warm and inviting approach to cooking, showcasing the best of Southern cuisine. Her passion for food, combined with her down-to-earth personality, has made her a beloved figure in the culinary world. With her signature Southern charm, Paula has managed to capture the essence of Southern baking and transform it into irresistible treats that will have you coming back for more.

In "Bite into the South," Paula Deen shares 98 of her most cherished baking recipes, each one a testament to the traditions and flavors that have shaped the South's culinary heritage. From Georgia to Louisiana, Alabama to Mississippi, this cookbook is a celebration of the region's rich culinary tapestry, encompassing both classic favorites and innovative creations inspired by the South's vibrant food culture.

The recipes in this cookbook are a reflection of Paula Deen's love for traditional Southern flavors, combined with her own unique twists. From the moment you open this book, you'll be greeted by the aroma of freshly baked goods and a sense of nostalgia that harkens back to a time when life was slower, and the kitchen was the heart of the home. Each recipe is accompanied by personal anecdotes and heartfelt stories, making this cookbook not just a collection of recipes, but also a glimpse into Paula's own Southern upbringing and the memories that have shaped her love for baking.

Whether you're an experienced baker or a novice in the kitchen, "Bite into the South" is designed to inspire and guide you through the art of Southern baking. From mastering the perfect flaky pie crust to achieving that melt-in-your-mouth texture in a cake, Paula's detailed instructions and helpful tips ensure that you'll be able to recreate these Southern delicacies with confidence and success.

As you explore the pages of this cookbook, you'll discover a wide array of recipes that cater to every palate and occasion. Indulge in the comforting sweetness of a classic pecan pie or savor the tangy flavors of a Key lime tart. Bake up a batch of buttery biscuits to accompany your morning coffee or surprise your loved ones with a stunning red velvet cake. With options ranging from quick and easy recipes to more elaborate creations, there's something for everyone in this collection.

But "Bite into the South" is more than just a cookbook—it's a celebration of Southern hospitality and the joy of sharing food with others. Paula Deen's warm and welcoming spirit shines through in every recipe, reminding us that the true pleasure of baking lies not just in the delicious results, but also in the joy it brings to our loved ones. From family gatherings to potluck dinners, these recipes are meant to be shared and savored with those who matter most.

So, grab your apron, preheat the oven, and get ready to embark on a culinary adventure that will transport you to the heart of the South. "Bite into the South: 98 Paula Deen's Baking Delights" is your invitation to experience the flavors, traditions, and warmth of Southern baking in your own kitchen. May these recipes bring you joy, create lasting memories, and leave you craving just one more bite of the South.

1. Red Velvet Cake

Red Velvet Cake is a delicious sponge cake with a velvety texture, topped with a rich and creamy cream cheese frosting. It's a classic dessert perfect for any occasion.
Serving: 12
Preparation Time: 25 minutes
Ready Time: 1 hour and 15 minutes

Ingredients:
- 2 ½ cups all-purpose flour
- 1 teaspoon baking soda
- 1 teaspoon salt
- 2 tablespoons cocoa powder
- 2 ¼ cups granulated sugar
- 2 eggs
- 1 ½ cups vegetable oil
- 1 cup buttermilk
- 1 tablespoon white vinegar
- 1 teaspoon vanilla extract
- 2 tablespoons liquid red food coloring
- 8 ounces cream cheese
- 4 tablespoons unsalted butter
- 2 ½ cups powdered sugar
- 1 teaspoon lemon juice

Instructions:
1. Preheat oven to 350°F. Grease and flour two 9-inch round cake pans.
2. In a medium bowl, mix flour, baking soda, salt, and cocoa powder.
3. In a large bowl, whisk together sugar, eggs, vegetable oil, buttermilk, vinegar, vanilla extract, and red food coloring until light and fluffy.
4. Gradually add the dry Ingredients to the wet Ingredients and mix until combined.
5. Divide the batter evenly between the two cake pans.
6. Bake for 30-35 minutes, or until a toothpick inserted into the center comes out clean. Let cool for 10 minutes in the pans before removing onto a wire cooling rack.

7. To make the frosting, cream together cream cheese and butter until light and fluffy. Gradually add in the powdered sugar, one cup at a time, while beating.
Mix in the lemon juice and mix until combined.
8. Ice the cake once completely cooled with the cream cheese frosting.

Nutrition information: Each serving contains approximate nutrition information: Calories:513, Fat: 22g, Saturated fat: 5g, Trans fat: 0g, Cholesterol: 41mg, Sodium: 370mg, Carbohydrates: 71g, Fiber: 1g, Sugars: 46g, Protein: 5g.

2. Pecan Pie

Pecan Pie is a classic American dessert made with a sweet and crunchy caramel-like filling surrounding a layer of roasted pecans, in a flaky pastry crust.
Serving: 8
Preparation Time: 15 minutes
Ready Time: 1 hour

Ingredients:
- ½ cup butter
- 1 cup light corn syrup
- ¾ cup granulated sugar
- 3 large eggs, beaten
- 1 teaspoon pure vanilla extract
- 2 cups pecans, chopped, toasted
- 1 9-inch unbaked pastry shell

Instructions:
1. Preheat oven to 350°F (175°C).
2. In a medium bowl, cream butter until light and fluffy.
3. Stir in corn syrup and sugar until blended. Add eggs, vanilla, and pecans; mix well.
4. Pour mixture into unbaked pastry shell.
5. Bake for 45-50 minutes or until golden brown; cool before serving.

Nutrition information: Calories: 563; Fat: 33g; Cholesterol: 75mg; Sodium: 145mg; Carbohydrates: 64g; Fiber: 2g; Protein: 5g.

3. Banana Pudding

This Banana Pudding is a creamy, delicious, and simple dessert that is sure to be a crowd-pleaser! Serve as a dessert or a snack, this recipe is easily adaptable to make for any occasion.
Serving: 8
Preparation Time: 20 minutes
Ready Time: 2 hours

Ingredients:
- 6–8 ripe bananas, peeled
- 2 packages (3.4 ounces each) instant vanilla pudding
- 5–6 cups milk
- 3 cups heavy cream
- 1/2 cup powdered sugar
- 2 teaspoons vanilla extract
- 1/2 teaspoon salt
- 1 package (14 ounces) graham crackers
- 1/4 cup melted butter

Instructions:
1. In a large bowl, whisk together the dry pudding mixes and 5 cups of milk until combined, about 1 minute.
2. Let the pudding rest for 5 minutes before adding the heavy cream, powdered sugar, vanilla extract, and salt.
3. Stir until well combined and set aside.
4. Grease a 9-x-13-inch baking dish with butter.
5. Layer the graham crackers and thinly sliced bananas in the dish.
6. Pour the pudding mixture over the top and spread evenly.
7. Sprinkle more graham crackers over the top.
8. Bake in preheated oven at 350°F for 15–20 minutes, or until the top is golden brown and the pudding is set.

Nutrition information: 1 Serving contains:
Calories: 373 kcal

Protein: 8.2g
Fat: 18.4g
Carbohydrates: 47.3g
Sugar: 25.4g
Fiber: 3.2g
Sodium: 275mg

4. Peach Cobbler

Peach Cobbler is a classic American summer dessert. A mixture of juicy, sweet peaches is cooked with a delicious biscuit-like topping that is crunchy on the outside and soft and fluffy on the inside. It's a perfect treat to enjoy after a summer BBQ.
Serving: 10
Preparation time: 30 minutes
Ready time: 60 minutes

Ingredients:
- 3 tablespoons butter
- 6 cups peeled and sliced fresh peaches
- 1 cup white sugar
- 1 teaspoon ground cinnamon
- 3 tablespoons all-purpose flour
- 1/2 teaspoon salt
- 1 cup all-purpose flour
- 1 tablespoon baking powder
- 3/4 cup white sugar
- 1/2 cup butter
- 3/4 cup milk

Instructions:
1. Preheat the oven to 350 degrees F (175 degrees C).
2. In a 9x13 inch baking dish, melt the butter.
3. Toss the sliced peaches with the sugar, cinnamon, flour, and salt, and spread over the melted butter in the baking dish.
4. In a medium bowl, mix the flour, baking powder, and sugar. Cut in the butter with a pastry blender or a fork until the mixture resembles coarse crumbs. Add the milk and mix until just blended.

5. Spread the crumb mixture evenly over the peaches.
6. Bake for 50 to 60 minutes, until the top is golden brown and the mixture is bubbly.

Nutrition information (per serving): 278 calories, 10.7 g fat, 0.5 g saturated fat, 35.4 g carbohydrates, 4.6 g protein, 2.2 g fibre, 86 mg sodium

5. Key Lime Pie

Key Lime Pie is a delicious dessert that combines tangy lime juice, rich sweet condensed milk, and a crunchy graham cracker crust. This classic pie is perfect for any occasion and sure to please the most picky of eaters.
Serving: 8
Preparation Time: 20 minutes
Ready Time: 3 hours (plus cooling time)

Ingredients:
- 1 (9-inch) prepared graham cracker crust
- 2 (14-ounce) cans sweetened condensed milk
- 1/2 cup key lime juice
- 3 egg yolks
- 2 teaspoons grated lime zest
- 1/4 teaspoon salt

Instructions:
1. Preheat oven to 350°F (175°C).
2. In a medium bowl, whisk together condensed milk, lime juice, egg yolks, lime zest, and salt until light and airy.
3. Pour the mixture into the graham cracker crust.
4. Bake for 15 minutes, or until the filling is set.
5. Let cool completely before refrigerating.
6. Refrigerate for at least 3 hours before serving.

Nutrition information: per serving- calories- 400, fat- 17g, saturated fat- 8g, cholesterol- 55 mg, sodium- 330 mg, carbohydrates- 47g, dietary fiber- 1g, sugars- 34g, protein- 6g

6. Buttermilk Biscuits

Buttermilk Biscuits are a classic, comforting biscuit that is perfect for a lazy Sunday morning or a side to a yummy dinner. Deliciously moist and flaky, these home-baked biscuits are sure to put a smile on your face.
Serving: This recipe makes about 10-12 biscuits.
Preparation time: The prep time for this recipe is 10 minutes.
Ready Time: The biscuits will take approximately 25 minutes to bake.

Ingredients:
- 2 cups All-purpose flour
- 2 tablespoons Sugar
- 1 tablespoon Baking powder
- 2 teaspoon Baking soda
- 1 teaspoon Salt
- 6 tablespoons Cold unsalted butter, cut into small cubes
- 2/3 cup Buttermilk

Instructions:
1. Preheat oven to 425°F (220°C).
2. In a large bowl, sift together the flour, sugar, baking powder, baking soda, and salt.
3. Cut the butter into the flour mixture until it resembles small pea-size bits.
4. Stir in the buttermilk until just combined.
5. Turn the dough out onto a lightly floured surface, and knead it 5–10 times.
6. Pat or roll the dough out to 1/2-inch thick.
7. Cut out biscuits using a biscuit cutter or a glass.
8. Place the biscuits onto a baking sheet lined with parchment paper.
9. Bake in preheated oven for 20–25 minutes, or until golden brown.

Nutrition information
Per 1 biscuit:
Calories - 102
Fat - 4.5 g
Cholesterol - 13mg

Sodium - 311 mg
Carbohydrates - 14.2 g
Sugars - 1.3 g
Protein - 2.2 g

7. Sweet Potato Pie

Sweet Potato Pie is a delicious, comforting, home-style dessert that's perfect for fall and winter celebrations.
Serving: 10
Preparation Time: 25 minutes
Ready Time: 1 hour 25 minutes

Ingredients:
- 1/2 cup dark-brown sugar
- 2 large eggs
- 1/4 cup butter, melted
- 2 teaspoons cornstarch
- 1/4 teaspoon ground cinnamon
- 1/2 teaspoon ground nutmeg
- 2 cups mashed cooked sweet potatoes
- 1/4 teaspoon salt
- 1 teaspoon vanilla extract
- 1 9-inch pie shell, unbaked

Instructions:
1. Preheat oven to 350 degrees.
2. In a medium bowl, beat together the brown sugar, eggs, and butter.
3. Add the cornstarch, cinnamon, nutmeg, mashed sweet potatoes, salt, and vanilla extract to the mixture.
4. Stir to combine.
5. Pour mixture into the unbaked pie shell.
6. Bake for 45 minutes, or until a toothpick inserted in the center comes out clean.
7. Let cool before serving.

Nutrition information: Serving Size: 1 slice (113 g), Calories: 217.6, Total Fat: 9.4 g, Saturated Fat: 3.7 g, Trans Fat: 0.2 g, Cholesterol:

41.4 mg, Sodium: 146.7 mg, Total Carbohydrate: 32.6 g, Dietary Fiber: 2.5 g, Sugars: 11.9 g, Protein: 3.1 g

8. Chocolate Chess Pie

Chocolate Chess Pie is an old-fashioned Southern dessert that is a blend of sweet and bitter chocolate with a creamy, custard-like texture. It is a long-standing favorite among those who adore chocolate.
Serving: 8
Preparation time: 20 minutes
Ready time: 1 hour 45 minutes

Ingredients:
- 3/4 cup all-purpose flour
- 1/4 teaspoon salt
- 1/4 teaspoon baking powder
- 2/3 cup granulated sugar
- 1 1/2 ounces unsweetened baking chocolate, finely chopped
- 4 tablespoons butter, melted
- 1/4 cup water
- 2 large eggs
- 2 tablespoons cornmeal
- 1 teaspoon pure vanilla extract
- 2 ounces semisweet baking chocolate, chopped
- 1 cup roughly chopped pecans
-1 deep dish frozen pie crust

Instructions:
1. Preheat the oven to 350 degrees F.
2. In a medium bowl, whisk together the flour, salt and baking powder.
3. In a separate bowl, whisk together the sugar, baking chocolate, butter, water, eggs, cornmeal and vanilla.
4. Pour the wet mixture into the flour mixture and mix until combined.
5. Stir in the chopped semisweet chocolate, pecans and frozen pie crust.
6. Pour the mixture into the pie crust.
7. Place the pie onto a baking sheet and bake for 1 hour and 45 minutes, or until the center is set and a toothpick inserted in the center comes out clean.

- 2 teaspoons vanilla extract
- 2 cups of water

Instructions:
1. Preheat oven to 350°F (176°C). Grease a 9x13 inch baking pan.
2. In a large bowl, mix together melted butter, cake mix, vanilla pudding mix, sugar, eggs, and vanilla extract until smooth. Stir in water. Pour into the greased baking pan.
3. Bake in preheated oven for 40 to 50 minutes, until a toothpick inserted into the center comes out clean. Allow to cool.

Nutrition information:
Calories: 223 kcal; Fat: 10g; Saturated Fat: 6g; Cholesterol: 73mg; Sodium: 315mg; Potassium: 97mg; Carbohydrates: 30g; Fiber: 0g; Sugar: 24g; Protein: 3g; Vitamin A: 368IU; Vitamin C: 0.9mg; Calcium: 50mg; Iron: 0.7mg

24. Blackberry Cobbler

Blackberry Cobbler is a wonderful traditional dessert that is often served during the summer. Perfectly sweet, with a crispy cobbled topping and a tarty, juicy blackberry filling on the bottom, this recipe is a must-try.
Serving: 8
Preparation Time: 10 minutes
Ready Time: 45 minutes

Ingredients:
- 4 cups fresh or frozen blackberries
- 3/4 cup sugar
- 2 tablespoons of cornstarch
- 1/4 teaspoon ground cinnamon
- 1/4 teaspoon ground nutmeg
- 1/4 teaspoon salt
- 3/4 cup (1 1/2 sticks) butter, melted
- 1 cup all-purpose flour
- 2 teaspoons baking powder
- 2/3 cup milk

Instructions:
1. Preheat oven to 375°F. Grease a 9x13-inch baking dish
2. In a medium bowl combine together the blackberries, sugar, cornstarch, cinnamon, nutmeg, and salt. Spread evenly in prepared baking dish.
3. Stir together melted butter, flour, and baking powder. Add milk and stir to combine, pour on top of the blackberry mixture.
4. Bake for 30-45 minutes, until lightly golden and bubbly. Serve with ice cream, if desired.

Nutrition information: Per serving: calories 278, fat 16.3 g, cholesterol 41 mg, sodium 265 mg, carbohydrates 33.4 g, dietary fiber 3.4 g, sugars 18.7 g, protein 2.6 g.

25. Buttermilk Pancakes

Buttermilk Pancakes are fluffy, creamy, yet tart and tangy. They are super easy to make and require few Ingredients, making them perfect for a family breakfast or brunch.
Serving: 8 pancakes.
Preparation Time: 15 minutes
Ready Time: 25 minutes

Ingredients:
- 1 cup all-purpose flour
- 2 tablespoons white sugar
- 2 teaspoons baking powder
- 1 teaspoon baking soda
- 1/4 teaspoon salt
- 1 cup buttermilk
- 2 tablespoons butter, melted
- 1 egg

Instructions:
1. In a large mixing bowl, combine the flour, sugar, baking powder, baking soda and salt.
2. In a separate bowl, whisk together the buttermilk, butter and egg.

3. Gradually add the wet Ingredients to the dry Ingredients, and stir until just combined.
4. Heat a lightly greased skillet over medium heat.
5. Scoop the batter onto the skillet in quarter-cup portions and cook until bubbly and golden. Flip each pancake and cook the other side for 1 minute or until golden.

Nutrition information
Per Serving (1 pancake):
Calories: 152
Total Fat: 5 g
Saturated Fat: 2.9 g
Cholesterol: 36 mg
Sodium: 286 mg
Carbohydrates: 22 g
Dietary Fiber: 0.8 g
Sugar: 6.3 g
Protein: 4.9 g

26. Hummingbird Cake

Hummingbird Cake is a traditional Southern concoction that comes in various forms. Known as "The Cake of the South," this cake is a delightful mix of spice, crushed pineapple, ripe bananas, and delicious pecans.
Serving: 8 to 10 people
Preparation Time: 30 minutes
Ready Time: 1 hour and 25 minutes

Ingredients:
- 2 cups all-purpose flour
- 1 teaspoon cinnamon
- 1 teaspoon baking soda
- 3 eggs
- 1 cup vegetable oil
- 2 cups sugar
- 1 teaspoon vanilla extract
- 1 8-ounce can crushed pineapple, drained

- 2 ripe bananas, mashed
- 1 cup chopped pecans

Instructions:
1. Preheat oven to 350°F. Grease and flour a 9 x 13-inch baking pan.
2. In a medium bowl, whisk together flour, cinnamon, baking soda, and salt; set aside.
3. In a large bowl, using an electric mixer, beat eggs, oil, and sugar until combined. Add in the vanilla extract.
4. Slowly add in the dry Ingredients, mixing until combined.
5. Fold in the pineapple, banana, and pecans.
6. Pour batter into prepared pan and bake for 45 to 50 minutes, or until a knife inserted in the center of the cake comes out clean.
7. Allow the cake to cool in the pan before serving.

Nutrition information:
Calories: 377 calories; Fat: 19.5g; Carbohydrates: 44.8g; Protein: 3.8g; Cholesterol: 39.2mg; Sodium: 169.8mg.

27. Fried Green Tomatoes

Fried Green Tomatoes is an amazing dish that combines the zestiness of tomatoes with the comforting crunch of fried batter. This dish is sure to tantalize your taste buds and delight your dinner guests.
Serving: 4
Preparation Time: 10 minutes
Ready Time: 20 minutes

Ingredients:
- 4 medium green tomatoes
- 1 large egg
- 1 cup all-purpose flour
- ¼ cup cornmeal
- 1 teaspoon garlic powder
- 1 teaspoon Italian seasoning
- Salt and pepper to taste
- ½ cup vegetable oil for frying

Instructions:
1. Cut tomatoes into ½ inch-thick slices.
2. In a shallow bowl, beat together egg and 1 tablespoon of water.
3. In another shallow bowl, mix together flour, cornmeal, garlic powder, Italian seasoning, salt and pepper.
4. Dip tomato slices into the egg mixture, then dredge in flour mixture.
5. Heat oil in a heavy skillet over medium-high heat.
6. Fry tomatoes in oil until golden brown and crisp.
7. Remove from skillet and drain on paper towels.

Nutrition information: Calories: 140; Total Fat: 10g; Saturated Fat: 7.3g; Cholesterol: 18mg; Sodium: 138mg; Carbohydrates: 10.6g; Protein: 2.7g

28. Bread Pudding

Bread pudding is a classic dessert that is made with day-old bread, dried fruits, and spices. It is often flavored with vanilla, cinnamon, and nutmeg and served warm with a dollop of cream or a drizzle of maple syrup. A delicious comfort food, it is the perfect way to finish off a meal.
Serving: 8
Preparation Time: 20 minutes
Ready Time: 1 hour

Ingredients:
- 5 cups day-old white bread, cubed
- 4 large eggs
- 2 cups whole milk
- 1/2 cup granulated sugar
- 2 tsp. ground cinnamon
- 1/2 tsp. ground nutmeg
- 2 tsp. pure vanilla extract
- 1/2 cup raisins (optional)

Instructions:
1. Preheat the oven to 350°F. Grease an 8-inch baking dish.
2. In a large bowl, whisk together the eggs, milk, sugar, cinnamon, nutmeg, and vanilla extract.

3. Add the cubed bread and mix until all the cubes are fully coated with the egg mixture.
4. Pour the mixture into the prepared baking dish and sprinkle the raisins on top (if using).
5. Bake for 40-45 minutes, or until the top is golden brown and the center is set.
6. Let cool for 15 minutes before serving.

Nutrition information:
Amount per Serving: • Calories: 238
- Fat: 6.1 g
- Saturated Fat: 2.5 g
- Trans Fat: 0 g
- Cholesterol: 103 mg
- Sodium: 225 mg
- Carbohydrates: 36.2 g
- Fiber: 1.3 g
- Sugar: 19.7 g
- Protein: 8.0 g

29. Southern Cornbread Dressing

Rich and flavorful, Southern Cornbread Dressing is the perfect addition to any holiday feast.
Serving: 6-8
Preparation time: 15 minutes
Ready time: 1 hour

Ingredients:
- 8 cups crumbled cornbread
- 2 tablespoons butter
- 2 celery stalks, chopped
- 1 onion, minced
- 2 cloves garlic, minced
- 2 eggs, beaten
- 2 cups chicken broth
- Salt and freshly ground black pepper, to taste

Instructions:
1. Preheat oven to 350 degrees F (175 degrees C).
2. Place crumbled cornbread in large bowl.
3. In a large skillet, melt butter over medium heat. Sauté celery, onion, and garlic until softened, about 5 minutes.
4. Add sautéed vegetables to cornbread.
5. In a small bowl, stir together eggs and chicken broth.
6. Pour egg and chicken broth mixture over cornbread and vegetables, stirring to combine everything.
7. Season with salt and pepper.
8. Grease a 9x13 inch baking dish and spread cornbread mixture evenly in the dish.
9. Bake in preheated oven for 45 minutes or until golden brown.

Nutrition information:
Calories: 175 kCal, Total Fat: 7g, Saturated Fat: 3g, Cholesterol: 64mg, Sodium: 447mg, Carbohydrates: 20g, Protein: 7g

30. Sweet Potato Casserole

Sweet Potato Casserole is a delicious traditional dish, which features sweet potatoes, butter, sugar, and spices. Perfectly balanced with a crunchy topping, this tasty side dish is welcomed by everyone who tries it.
Serving: Serves 8-10
Preparation time: 15 minutes
Ready time: 1 hour

Ingredients:
- 4 cups of mashed sweet potatoes
- 1/2 cup of butter, melted
- 1 cup of white sugar
- 1 teaspoon of vanilla extract
- 2 eggs, lightly beaten
- 1/2 cup of milk
- 1/2 cup of brown sugar
- 1/2 cup of chopped pecans

Instructions:
1. Preheat oven to 350 degrees F (175 degrees C). Grease a 9x13 inch baking dish.
2. In a large bowl, mix together mashed sweet potatoes, melted butter, white sugar, and vanilla. Stir in eggs and milk until the mixture is well blended. Spread the mixture into the prepared baking dish.
3. In a small bowl, mix together the brown sugar and chopped pecans. Sprinkle the mixture over the sweet potatoes.
4. Bake for 40 to 50 minutes in the preheated oven, until topping is golden brown.

Nutrition information: Per serving: 290 calories; 10.9 g fat; 47.2 g carbohydrates; 4.1 g protein; 49 mg cholesterol; 77 mg sodium.

31. Apple Pie

Apple Pie is an all-time favorite treat made with a buttery, flaky crust filled with a tart-sweet apples filling.
Serving: 8
Preparation time: 45 minutes
Ready time: 1 hour

Ingredients:
- 2 9-inch unbaked pie crust
- 7 cups peeled, sliced apples
- 1 cup white sugar
- 1/3 cup all-purpose flour
- 1 teaspoon ground cinnamon
- ½ teaspoon salt
- 1 tablespoon lemon juice
- 2 tablespoons butter

Instructions:
1. Preheat oven to 425 degrees F.
2. Line 9-inch pie dish with one pie crust, trimming off any excess.
3. In a large bowl, combine apples, sugar, flour, cinnamon, salt, and lemon juice. Mix together until all Ingredients are evenly distributed.
4. Pour into prepared pie dish. Dot with butter.

5. Cover with top crust, pressing edges together to seal.
6. Bake for 40 to 45 minutes, or until crust is golden brown.

Nutrition information: per serving: Calories 330, Total Fat 11.6g, Saturated Fat 5.7g, Cholesterol 16.5mg, Sodium 204mg, Total Carbohydrate 55.3g, Dietary Fiber 3.8g, Protein 2.9g.

32. Butter Pecan Ice Cream

Butter Pecan Ice Cream is creamy and delicious, made with toasty pecans and warm butter that accents the great taste of vanilla.
Serving: Makes 8 servings
Preparation Time: 15 minutes
Ready Time: 4 hours or overnight

Ingredients:
2 cups heavy cream; 1/2 cup granulated sugar; 2 tablespoon light corn syrup; pinch salt; 2 tablespoons pure vanilla extract; 1/2 cup pecans; 2 tablespoons butter

Instructions:
1. In a medium bowl, whisk together the heavy cream and sugar until the sugar is completely dissolved.
2. Stir in the corn syrup and salt until fully combined.
3. Add in the vanilla extract and mix to combine.
4. Toast the pecans in a sauté pan over medium heat, for about 5 minutes or until lightly toasted.
5. Add the butter to the pan and melt until completely combined with the pecans.
6. Pour the cream mixture into the pan and stir until evenly combined.
7. Let the mixture cool to room temperature.
8. Transfer the mixture to an ice cream maker and churn according to manufacturers directions.
9. Once finished, transfer the ice cream to a freezer-safe container and freeze for at least 4 hours or overnight.

Nutrition information: Calories: 95; Fat: 5.6 g; Saturated Fat: 3.4 g; Cholesterol: 17 mg; Sodium: 24 mg; Carbohydrates: 10.9 g; Fiber: 0.3 g; Sugar: 9.5 g; Protein: 1.3 g.

33. Baked Macaroni and Cheese

Baked Macaroni and Cheese is an easy and delicious way to satisfy your craving for something cheesy and comforting. It's creamy, cheesy and simplymouth-watering!
Serving: 6
Preparation time: 15 minutes
Ready time: 1 hour

Ingredients:
- 16 oz elbow macaroni
- 4 tablespoons butter
- 4 tablespoons all-purpose flour
- 3 cups milk
- 2 cups grated sharp cheddar cheese
- 1 teaspoon dry mustard
- 1 teaspoon salt

Instructions:
1. Preheat the oven to 350°F. Grease a 9 x 13-inch baking dish.
2. Cook macaroni according to package directions until al dente. Do not overcook.
3. In a medium saucepan, melt the butter over medium heat. Stir in the flour and cook for 2 minutes. Gradually add the milk, whisking constantly. Continue to cook for an additional 5 minutes or until the mixture is thick and bubbly.
4. Remove from the heat and stir in the cheese, mustard, and salt.
5. Pour the cooked macaroni into the prepared baking dish, then pour the cheese sauce over top. Stir to combine.
6. Cover with aluminum foil and bake in preheated oven for 25 minutes. Uncover and bake for an additional 25 minutes or until the top is lightly golden brown.

Nutrition information:

- Calories: 458
- Total Fat: 21 g
- Saturated Fat: 13 g
- Cholesterol: 55 mg
- Sodium: 704 mg
- Total Carbohydrates: 43 g
- Dietary Fiber: 2 g
- Sugars: 8 g
- Protein: 19 g

34. Gooey Butter Cake

Gooey Butter Cake is a classic dessert from St. Louis, Missouri that has a soft and creamy texture. It is popular among adults and children alike.
Serving: 8-10
Preparation Time: 15 minutes
Ready Time: 55 minutes

Ingredients:
-1/2 cup butter, melted
-1 box yellow cake mix
-1 egg
-1 teaspoon vanilla extract
-8 ounces cream cheese, softened
-1/4 cup butter, softened
-1/2 teaspoon almond extract
-2 eggs
-1/2 cup sour cream
-3 tablespoons cornstarch
-8 ounces cream cheese, softened
-1/2 cup butter, softened
-3 tablespoons sugar

Instructions:
1. Preheat oven to 350°F. Grease a 9x13-inch baking pan.
2. In a medium bowl, add the melted butter, cake mix, egg, and vanilla extract. Mix until the Ingredients are combined.

3. Press the the cake mix mixture into the bottom of the prepared pan and set aside to cool.
4. In a separate bowl, add the cream cheese, butter, almond extract, eggs, and sour cream. Beat until the Ingredients are combined.
5. Add the cornstarch and sugar and mix until combined.
6. Pour the cream cheese mixture over the prepared cake mix mixture. Spread over the top evenly.
7. Bake for 45 minutes, or until the top is golden brown and the center is set.
8. Let cool before serving.

Nutrition information: Calories: 183, Carbohydrates: 14g, Protein: 2g, Fat: 14g, Saturated Fat: 8g, Cholesterol: 68mg, Sodium: 192mg, Potassium: 23mg, Fiber: 0g, Sugar: 10g, Vitamin A: 510IU, Calcium: 58mg, Iron: 0.4mg

35. Fried Chicken and Waffles

Fried chicken and waffles is a classic combination of savoury and sweet flavours. It is a popular brunch dish that is served in many restaurants throughout the United States. Crisp fried chicken is served atop a waffle, usually topped with butter and syrup for an amazing combination of flavours.
Serving: Makes 4 servings
Preparation time: 20 minutes
Ready Time: 45 minutes

Ingredients:
- 4 skinless and boneless chicken breasts
- 2 eggs
- 2 cups all purpose flour
- 2 tablespoons garlic powder
- 2 tablespoons paprika
- 1 teaspoon salt
- 2 tablespoon ground black pepper
- Canola oil for frying
- 2 cups prepared waffles
- Butter and syrup for serving (optional)

Instructions:
1. Preheat oven to 375°F (190°C).
2. In a shallow bowl, beat the eggs until combined.
3. In a separate shallow bowl, combine the flour, garlic powder, paprika, salt, and pepper.
4. Dip the chicken breasts in the egg mixture, then coat in the flour mixture.
5. Heat a large skillet over medium heat with enough oil to cover the bottom of the pan.
6. Fry the chicken breasts until golden and crisp, about 5 minutes per side. Transfer to a baking sheet and bake in the preheated oven until the chicken is cooked through, about 15 minutes.
7. Serve the fried chicken on top of the prepared waffles with butter and syrup.

Nutrition information
Calories: 500, Fat: 24g, Carbohydrates: 80g, Protein: 48g

36. Cheese Straws

Cheese Straws is a tasty and crispy treat which is made with cheese, butter, and flour. It is easy to make and is great for sharing with friends and family.
Serving: Makes about 30 pieces
Preparation Time: 15 minutes
Ready Time: 1 hour

Ingredients:
- 4 ounces cheddar cheese, grated
- 4 tablespoons butter
- 1 cup all-purpose flour
- Pinch of salt
- A few grindings of black pepper
- 2 teaspoons smoked paprika

Instructions:
1. Preheat oven to 350°F.

2. Mix together the grated cheese and butter in a bowl.
3. Add the flour, salt, and pepper, and paprika, and mix until the mixture forms a dough.
4. On a work surface, roll the dough into a long log about 1 inch in diameter.
5. Using a sharp knife, cut the log into 1-inch pieces.
6. Arrange the pieces on a baking sheet and bake for 12 minutes.
7. Let cool and serve.

Nutrition information:
Calories: 55
Fat: 3 g
Carbohydrates: 5 g
Protein: 2 g

37. Strawberry Rhubarb Pie

This deliciously, sweet and tart Strawberry Rhubarb Pie is a great summertime treat.
Serving: Makes 8 servings
Preparation time: 30 minutes
Ready time: 1 1/2 hours

Ingredients:
1 prepared pie crust
2 to 3 cups sliced fresh rhubarb
2 to 3 cups sliced fresh strawberries
3/4 cup granulated sugar
4 tablespoons all-purpose flour
1/4 teaspoon ground cinnamon
1 tablespoon butter

Instructions:
1. Preheat oven to 400°F.
2. Place prepared pie crust in 9-inch pie plate.
3. Combine rhubarb and strawberries in a mixing bowl.
4. Add the sugar, flour, and cinnamon to the bowl, and stir gently to combine.

5. Place the mixture in the prepared pie crust.
6. Dot the top with the butter.
7. Place the top crust over the filling.
8. Crimp the edges together with your hands.
9. Cut several steam vents in the top.
10. Bake the pie for 50 to 60 minutes until crust is golden brown and filling is bubbly.
11. Allow to cool before cutting.

Nutrition information:
Serving size: 1 slice
Calories: 265
Total Fat: 9.3g
Cholesterol: 0mg
Sodium: 154mg
Total Carbohydrate: 44.7g
Protein: 2.5g

38. Old-Fashioned Chocolate Layer Cake

This classic old-fashioned recipe for Old-Fashioned Chocolate Layer Cake will make everyone reach for seconds. With its moist dark chocolate layers, fluffy frosting, and heavenly aroma, this cake is sure to be the life of the party.
Serving: Serves 10-12
Preparation time: 15 minutes
Ready time: 2 hours

Ingredients:
- 2 ½ cups self-rising flour
- 4 tablespoons cocoa powder
- 2 ½ cups granulated sugar
- 1 cup (2 sticks) unsalted butter, softened
- 4 large eggs
- 1 cup buttermilk
- 2 teaspoons pure vanilla extract
- 1 cup boiling water

Instructions:
1. Preheat oven to 350°F. Grease and flour two 9-inch round cake pans.
2. In a medium bowl, whisk together the flour and cocoa powder; set aside.
3. In a large bowl, beat the butter and sugar together until light and fluffy.
4. Add in the eggs, one at a time, until fully incorporated into the butter mixture.
5. Beat in the buttermilk and vanilla extract.
6. Slowly beat in the flour mixture until a thick batter forms.
7. Beat in the boiling water until the batter is smooth.
8. Divide the batter evenly between the two prepared pans.
9. Bake in the preheated oven for 35-40 minutes or until a toothpick inserted in the middle comes out clean.
10. Let cool in the pans for 15 minutes before transferring to a cooling rack.

Nutrition information: Calories: 307, Fat: 14.5g, Saturated fat: 8.2g, Carbohydrates: 41.3g, Sugar: 27.2g, Protein: 4.3g, Fiber: 0.7g, Cholesterol: 77.2mg, Sodium: 229.6mg

39. Chicken and Dumplings

Chicken and Dumplings is a delicious, comforting dish of succulent dumplings cooked in flavorful chicken broth.
Serving: 8
Preparation Time: 10 minutes
Ready Time: 25 minutes

Ingredients:
- 8 cups chicken broth
- 2 cups cooked shredded chicken
- 1 (10-ounce) can refrigerated biscuit dough, cut into small pieces
- 2 tablespoons butter
- 1 onion, chopped
- 2 tablespoons all-purpose flour
- Salt and freshly ground black pepper, to taste
- 2 tablespoons chopped fresh parsley

Instructions:
1. In a large pot, bring the chicken broth to a boil over high heat.
2. Add the chicken and biscuit dough. Reduce the heat to low and simmer for 15 minutes, stirring occasionally.
3. In a separate skillet, melt the butter over medium heat. Add the onion and sauté for 3 minutes. Add the flour, salt, and pepper and cook for an additional minute.
4. Add the onion mixture to the pot and simmer for 5 more minutes.
5. Stir in the parsley and serve.

Nutrition information: Calories: 177, Protein: 13.3 grams, Fat: 6.7 grams, Fiber: 0.9 gram, Cholesterol: 24 milligrams, Sodium: 580 milligrams, Carbohydrates: 16.1 grams

40. Lemon Meringue Pie

Lemon Meringue Pie is an iconic dessert that's been a beloved staple of American cooking for centuries. Its combination of tart lemon filling and airy meringue topping is sure to tantalize taste buds over any gathering!
Serving: Serves 8
Preparation Time: 15 minutes
Ready Time: 2 hours

Ingredients:
- 2 cup sugar
- ¼ cup cornstarch
- ½ cup all-purpose flour
- ¼ teaspoon salt
- 1 ¼ cup cold water
- 2 tablespoons butter
- 2 tablespoons grated lemon zest
- 2/3 cup fresh lemon juice
- 3 eggs, separated
- 1 unbaked 9-inch pie crust

Instructions:

1. In a medium saucepan, whisk together the sugar, cornstarch, flour and salt. Gradually whisk in the cold water until smooth.
2. Heat the mixture over medium-high heat, whisking constantly, until it comes to a boil. Boil for 1 minute, then reduce the heat to low.
3. Add the butter, lemon zest and lemon juice and stir until fully combined.
4. In a separate bowl, beat the egg whites until stiff peaks form.
5. Pour the hot lemon mixture into the pie crust and spread the egg whites over the top.
6. Bake at 375°F for 30-35 minutes, or until the meringue is golden brown. Allow to cool to room temperature before serving.

Nutrition information:
Per serving: 203 calories, 6.3 g fat, 36 g carbohydrates, 3.3 g protein, 64 mg sodium, 43 mg cholesterol

41. Coca-Cola Cake

Coca-Cola Cake is a unique and flavorful dessert that combines the sweet iconic flavor of Coca-Cola with a rich and delicious cake.
Serving: 9-12
Preparation time: 10 minutes
Ready time: 40 minutes

Ingredients:
- 2 cups all-purpose flour
- 2 cups granulated sugar
- 1 teaspoon baking soda
- ½ teaspoon salt
- 1 cup Coca Cola
- ½ cup vegetable oil
- 2 tablespoons cocoa powder
- 2 eggs
- ½ cup buttermilk

Instructions:
1. Preheat the oven to 350 degrees F. Lightly grease a 9x13 baking dish.

2. In a large bowl, whisk together the flour, sugar, baking soda, salt, and cocoa powder.
3. In a separate bowl, whisk together the Coca Cola, oil, eggs, and buttermilk.
4. Pour the wet Ingredients into the bowl with the dry Ingredients and stir until combined.
5. Pour the batter into the prepared baking dish and bake for 40 minutes or until the top springs back when lightly pressed.
6. Allow the cake to cool before serving.
Nutrition Info: Per serving: Calories: 384, Protein: 4 g, Fat: 15 g, Carbs: 56 g, Fiber: 1 g, Sugar: 32 g

42. Buttermilk Fried Shrimp

Buttermilk Fried Shrimp is a tasty dish that is sure to keep everyone coming back for more! It is bursting with salty and creamy flavors, and it's the perfect appetizer or main dish.
Serving: 6-8
Preparation time: 10 minutes
Ready time: 25 minutes

Ingredients:
- 1 pound large shrimp, peeled and deveined
- 1 cup buttermilk
- 1 cup all-purpose flour
- 2 teaspoons garlic powder
- 1 teaspoon paprika
- Salt and pepper to taste
- 1 cup vegetable oil

Instructions:
1. In a shallow bowl, combine the buttermilk and shrimp. Cover and refrigerate for 10 minutes.
2. In a separate shallow bowl, whisk together the flour, garlic powder, paprika, and a generous pinch each of salt and pepper.
3. Heat the oil in a large skillet over medium heat.
4. Take the shrimp out of the buttermilk, and dip in the flour until it is completely coated.

5. Place the shrimp in the hot oil, and cook for about two minutes per side, or until golden brown.
6. Remove from heat and drain on a paper towel-lined plate.

Nutrition information: Serving size: 1/8 of recipe (4 shrimp), Calories: 268, Carbs: 14g, Protein: 16g, Fat: 15g, Saturated Fat: 8g, Sodium: 590mg, Cholesterol: 170mg, Fiber: 0g, Sugar: 0g.

43. Peach Ice Cream

Enjoy a delicious, homemade peach ice cream with this easy recipe. It makes a great sweet treat for summer and for special occasions.
Serving: 8 servings
Preparation time: 10 minutes
Ready Time: 4 hours

Ingredients:
- 2 cups heavy cream
- 2 cups half-and-half
- 1 (14-ounce) can sweetened condensed milk
- 2 teaspoons vanilla extract
- 2 tablespoons almond extract
- 1/4 teaspoon salt
- 4 large ripe peaches, peeled, pitted, and chopped

Instructions:
1. In a large bowl, stir together heavy cream, half-and-half, sweetened condensed milk, vanilla extract, almond extract, and salt until well blended.
2. Add chopped peaches to the cream mixture and stir to combine.
3. Transfer the mixture to an ice cream maker and freeze according to manufacturer's instructions.
4. Place the freshly churned ice cream in an air-tight container and freeze until firmly set, about 4 hours.

Nutrition information: Serving size: 1/8 of recipe, Calories: 470, Fat: 26g, Saturated fat: 15g, Cholesterol: 97mg, Sodium: 131mg, Carbohydrates: 43g, Fiber: 1g, Protein: 9g

44. Biscuit Cinnamon Rolls

Biscuit Cinnamon Rolls are an easy and delicious way to enjoy the classic flavor of cinnamon rolls without having to wait for the dough to rise! A combination of biscuit dough and cinnamon sugar creates a buttery, sweet and gooey treat that will surely be enjoyed by all.
Serving: 8
Preparation Time : 5 minutes
Ready Time : 15 minutes

Ingredients:
- 2 cans refrigerated biscuit dough
- ½ cup butter, melted
- 2 teaspoons ground cinnamon
- ¼ cup light brown sugar
- ½ cup chopped nuts (optional)

Instructions:
1. Preheat oven to 350°F (177°C). Grease a 9×13-inch baking dish.
2. Open the cans of biscuit dough. Cut each biscuit into 8 equal pieces.
3. In a medium bowl, combine melted butter, cinnamon, and brown sugar.
4. Dip each biscuit piece into the butter mixture, coating both sides and then placing in the greased baking dish.
5. Sprinkle nuts, if desired, over the top of the biscuit pieces.
6. Bake in preheated oven for 15 minutes or until golden brown.

Nutrition information:
Each serving (1 biscuit cinnamon roll) contains approximately 115 calories, 6g fat, 11g carbohydrates, 1g protein and 1g fiber.

45. Sweet Potato Biscuits

Sweet Potato Biscuits are a quick and easy sweet snack made with mashed sweet potato, butter, eggs, and sugar. They are perfect for dipping in coffee or tea.

Serving: Makes 12 biscuits
Preparation Time: 10 minutes
Ready Time: 20 minutes

Ingredients:
- 2 cups mashed sweet potato
- 1/4 cup sugar
- 6 tablespoons butter, melted
- 2 large eggs
- 2 cups all-purpose flour

Instructions:
1. Preheat oven to 375F (190C).
2. In a large bowl, mix together the mashed sweet potato, sugar, melted butter, and eggs until combined.
3. Add the flour and mix until a dough forms.
4. Using a cookie scoop or spoon, scoop dough and shape into 12 equal-sized balls. Place on a baking sheet lined with parchment paper.
5. Bake for 18-20 minutes, or until golden brown.
6. Let cool before serving.

Nutrition information per biscuit:
Calories: 115
Fat: 4 g
Carbohydrates: 16 g
Protein: 3 g

46. Lemon Poppy Seed Bread

Lemon Poppy Seed Bread is a sweet and zesty treat with a crunchy poppy seed topping. This easy-to-make recipe features tart lemon juice and zest, and comes together in no time.
Serving: 12 slices
Preparation time: 10 minutes
Ready time: 50 minutes

Ingredients:
- 2¼ cups all-purpose flour

- ¼ teaspoon baking soda
- 2 teaspoons baking powder
- ½ teaspoon salt
- 3 tablespoons poppy seeds
- ¾ cup granulated sugar
- ¼ cup butter, softened
- 1 teaspoon lemon zest
- 2 eggs
- ½ cup Greek yogurt
- 1 teaspoon pure vanilla extract
- ¼ cup freshly squeezed lemon juice

Instructions:
1. Preheat your oven to 350°F (176°C) and prepare a 9x5-inch loaf pan with non-stick cooking spray.
2. In a medium bowl, whisk together the flour, baking soda, baking powder, salt, and poppy seeds. Set aside.
3. In the bowl of a stand mixer, beat together the sugar and butter until light and fluffy.
4. Mix in the lemon zest, eggs, yogurt, and vanilla until fully combined.
5. Mix in the dry Ingredients until just combined.
6. Gently fold in the lemon juice.
7. Pour the batter into the prepared loaf pan and bake for 45-50 minutes, until a toothpick inserted into the center comes out clean.
8. Let the bread cool in the pan for 10 minutes, then turn out onto a wire rack to cool completely.

Nutrition information:
Calories: 204, Total Fat: 7g, Saturated Fat: 4g, Trans Fat: 0g, Cholesterol: 46mg, Sodium: 205mg, Carbohydrates: 30g, Fiber: 1g, Sugar: 14g, Protein: 5g

47. Hush Puppies

Hush puppies are tasty and crunchy fried cornmeal balls that are typically served as a side dish. They are a traditional staple of the Southern United States, but their popularity has spread far and wide.

Serving: Hush puppies are typically enjoyed as part of a meal with other sides. It's often served with fish or seafood but can be served as an accompaniment to many other main dishes.
Preparation time: 10 minutes
Ready time: 15 minutes

Ingredients:
- 1 cup cornmeal
- 1/4 cup all-purpose flour
- 1/4 teaspoon baking powder
- 1 teaspoon sugar
- 1/4 teaspoon baking soda
- 1/2 teaspoon salt
- 1/4 cup finely chopped onion
- 3/4 cup buttermilk
- 1/4 cup melted butter
- Vegetable oil, for frying

Instructions:
1. In a medium bowl, combine the cornmeal, flour, baking powder, sugar, baking soda, and salt.
2. Stir in the onion, then slowly add the buttermilk and melted butter, stirring until just combined.
3. Heat 1/3-inch of vegetable oil in a cast-iron skillet over medium-high heat.
4. Drop tablespoon-size balls of the batter into the oil.
5. Fry for 3 minutes per side, or until golden brown and crisp.
6. Remove from the oil and let drain on a paper towel-lined plate.

Nutrition information: per serving, approximately 97 calories, 5.5g fat, 9.2g carbohydrates, 1.7g protein.

48. Southern Banana Bread

This Southern Banana Bread is a sweet and moist quick bread, flavorful with chopped pecans and banana.
Serving: Serves 8-10.
Preparation time: 15 minutes

Ready time: 1 hour 10 minutes

Ingredients:
- 2 cups all-purpose flour
- 1 teaspoon baking powder
- 1 teaspoon baking soda
- 1 teaspoon ground cinnamon
- 1/4 teaspoon salt
- 3 ripe bananas
- 1/4 cup melted butter
- 1 teaspoon vanilla extract
- 2 eggs
- 1 cup sugar
- 1/2 cup chopped pecans

Instructions:
1. Preheat the oven to 350°F. Grease and lightly flour a 9"x5" loaf pan.
2. In a medium bowl, whisk together the flour, baking powder, baking soda, cinnamon, and salt.
3. In a large bowl, mash the bananas with a fork.
4. Add the melted butter, vanilla extract, eggs, sugar and mix until combined.
5. Stir in the mashed bananas and stir in the dry Ingredients until just combined.
6. Fold in the chopped pecans.
7. Pour the batter into the greased and floured loaf pan.
8. Bake for 50-60 minutes, or until a wooden skewer inserted in the center comes out clean.
9. Allow to cool in the pan for 10 minutes before transferring to a wire cooling rack.

Nutrition information: 269 calories, 11.5 g fat, 2.4 g saturated fat, 41.3 g total carbohydrate, 2.1 g protein.

49. Apple Fritters

Apple Fritters are delicious, crispy morsels packed with juicy apples and lightly dusted in cinnamon sugar. The perfect breakfast or dessert!

Serving: 4
Preparation Time: 10 mins
Ready Time: 25 mins

Ingredients:
-1 cup all purpose flour
-2 tablespoons granulated sugar
-1/2 teaspoon baking powder
-1/4 teaspoon salt
-1/2 teaspoon ground cinnamon
-2 tablespoons milk
-1 large egg
-1 teaspoon pure vanilla extract
-2 medium apples, peeled and finely diced
-1/4 cup canola oil, or other frying oil
-Extra granulated sugar, for dusting

Instructions:
1. In a large bowl, whisk together the flour, sugar, baking powder, salt, and ground cinnamon.
2. In a separate bowl, whisk together the milk, egg, and vanilla extract.
3. Pour the wet Ingredients over the dry Ingredients and stir to combine.
4. Add the diced apples into the batter and gently mix until evenly distributed.
5. Heat the oil in a large skillet over medium heat.
6. Scoop the batter with a spoon and carefully drop into the hot oil.
7. Cook for 2-3 minutes, or until golden brown on each side.
8. Transfer the fritters to a plate lined with paper towels to drain off any extra oil.
9. Sprinkle with granulated sugar and serve warm.

Nutrition information:
Serving size: 1 fritter
Calories: 150
Fat: 7 g
Carbohydrates: 19 g
Protein: 3 g

50. Cinnamon Sugar Donuts

Try out this delicious and easy-to-follow Cinnamon Sugar Donut Recipe and enjoy light and crispy donuts coated in a perfect cinnamon sugar mix.
Serving: Makes 12 donuts
Preparation Time: 25 minutes
Ready Time: 10 minutes

Ingredients:
- 2 ½ cups all-purpose flour
- ⅓ cup granulated sugar
- 2 teaspoons baking powder
- ½ teaspoon baking soda
- ½ teaspoon salt
- 1 teaspoon cinnamon
- 2 large eggs
- 1 ½ cups buttermilk
- 4 tablespoons melted butter
- 2 teaspoons vanilla extract
- Vegetable oil, for frying
- Cinnamon sugar mix, for coating

Instructions:
1. In a bowl, mix together the flour, sugar, baking powder, baking soda, salt, and cinnamon, then set aside.
2. In a separate bowl, whisk together the eggs, buttermilk, melted butter, and vanilla extract until well combined.
3. Add the wet Ingredients to the dry Ingredients and mix until just combined.
4. Cover the bowl with plastic wrap and let the dough rest for 15 minutes.
5. In a large pot over medium-high heat, heat the vegetable oil to 350°F (175°C).
6. On a lightly floured surface roll out the dough to ½-inch thickness.
7. Cut out the donuts using a 3-inch biscuit cutter.
8. Carefully add the donuts, a few at a time, to the hot oil. Fry the donuts for 30 seconds to 1 minute per side, or until golden brown.
9. Using a slotted spoon, transfer the donuts to a cooling rack.
10. Once cooled, coat the donuts in the cinnamon sugar mix.

Nutrition information: Per Serving- Calories: 304, Fat: 9g, Saturated Fat: 5g, Cholesterol: 46mg, Sodium: 245mg, Carbohydrates: 47g, Fiber: 1g, Sugar: 18g, Protein: 6g

51. Strawberry Jam Thumbprint Cookies

Enjoy these delicious Strawberry Jam Thumbprint Cookies. They are easy to make and taste great.
Serving: Makes 12 cookies.
Preparation Time: 15 minutes.
Ready Time: 45 minutes.

Ingredients:
- 1/2 cup butter, softened
- 1/2 cup sugar
- 1/2 teaspoon vanilla extract
- 1 large egg
- 1/2 teaspoon baking powder
- 1/4 teaspoon salt
- 1 cup all-purpose flour
- 1/4 cup strawberry jam

Instructions:
1. Preheat oven to 375°F. Line a baking sheet with parchment paper or a silicone baking mat; set aside.
2. In a medium bowl, using a hand mixer, beat together butter and sugar until light and fluffy. Beat in vanilla extract and egg.
3. In a separate bowl, mix together baking powder, salt, and flour. Slowly add flour mixture to butter mixture and mix until combined.
4. Using a spoon or cookie scoop, scoop out 12 balls of dough onto the prepared baking sheet. Gently flatten each dough ball and make a thumbprint in the center of each cookie.
5. Place a teaspoon of strawberry jam in the thumbprint of each cookie. Bake for 15 minutes, or until edges are golden brown.
6. Allow cookies to cool on baking sheet for 5 minutes before transferring to a wire rack to cool completely.

Nutrition information: Per 1 cookie – Calories: 114, Fat: 5 g, Cholesterol: 18 mg, Sodium: 81 mg, Carbohydrates: 14 g, Fiber: 0 g, Sugar: 6 g, Protein: 1 g

52. Coconut Cream Pie

Rich and creamy Coconut Cream Pie is a classic American dessert made with a homemade coconut-infused custard-like filling and piled high with freshly whipped cream and grated coconut.
Serving: 8
Preparation Time: 25 minutes
Ready Time: 2 hours

Ingredients:
- 1 9-inch pie crust
- 1 14-ounce can of coconut milk
- 2 large eggs
- 1/2 cup granulated sugar
- 1/4 cup all-purpose flour
- 1/4 teaspoon salt
- 1/4 teaspoon nutmeg
- 1 teaspoon coconut extract
- Topping:
- 1/2 cup heavy cream
- 2 tablespoons confectioners' sugar
- 2 tablespoons toasted coconut

Instructions:
1. Pre-heat the oven to 350°F and place the pre-made or pre-baked pie crust into a 9-inch pie pan.
2. In a medium size bowl, whisk the coconut milk, eggs, sugar, flour, salt, nutmeg and coconut extract until the mixture is fully combined.
3. Pour the mixture into the prepared pie crust.
4. Bake the pie for about 25 minutes, or until set.
5. Allow the pie to cool completely before topping with whipped cream and toasted coconut.
6. To make the topping, add heavy cream and confectioners' sugar to a bowl and whisk together until stiff peaks form.

7. Spread the whipped cream over the cooled pie and top with the toasted coconut.

Nutrition information: Per Serving – Calories: 320; Fat: 17g; Cholesterol: 53mg; Sodium: 246mg; Carbohydrates: 37g; Protein: 4g

53. Praline Pecan Bread Pudding

Indulge in the simple pleasure of Praline Pecan Bread Pudding, a comforting Southern-style dessert. Moist and rich, it's made with egg-soaked cubes of bread and a praline pecan topping.
Serving: Serves 8
Preparation time: 25 minutes
Ready time: 1 hour 35 minutes

Ingredients:
4 cups diced day-old white bread
2 tablespoons butter
3 eggs
2 tablespoons cornstarch
2 cups whole milk
2 teaspoons vanilla
1/3 cup granulated sugar
1/3 cup packed brown sugar
1 teaspoon ground cinnamon
Praline Pecan Topping:
1/3 cup packed brown sugar
2 tablespoons butter, melted
1/2 cup chopped pecans
1/3 cup all-purpose flour

Instructions:
1. Preheat oven to 350°F. Grease an 8-inch baking dish.
2. Place the bread cubes in the prepared baking dish and dot with butter.
3. In a medium bowl, whisk together eggs, cornstarch, milk, vanilla, sugars and cinnamon; pour over the bread cubes in the baking dish; let stand for 15 minutes.

4. In a medium bowl, combine the brown sugar, butter, pecans and flour for the topping; sprinkle over the pudding.
5. Bake for 40–45 minutes until golden and set.

Nutrition information:
Per serving: 238 calories; 11 g fat; 2 g saturated fat; 41 mg cholesterol; 164 mg sodium; 34 g carbohydrate; 2 g fiber; 19 g sugar; 5 g protein.

54. Brown Sugar Pecan Cookies

Brown sugar pecan cookies are a delightfully crunchy and sweet treat that is sure to be a hit with the whole family. Serve with milk or coffee and enjoy!
Serving: Makes 18 cookies
Preparation time: 15 minutes
Ready time: 45 minutes

Ingredients:
- 1 cup butter, softened
- 3/4 cup packed light brown sugar
- 1/2 cup granulated sugar
- 2 large eggs
- 2 teaspoons vanilla extract
- 2-1/4 cups all-purpose flour
- 1 teaspoon baking soda
- 1/4 teaspoon salt
- 1-1/2 cups coarsely chopped pecans

Instructions:
1. Preheat oven to 350°. In a large bowl, cream butter and sugars until light and fluffy. Beat in eggs and vanilla. In another bowl, whisk flour, baking soda and salt; gradually beat into creamed mixture. Stir in pecans.
2. Drop by tablespoonfuls 2 in. apart onto ungreased baking sheets. Bake 12-14 minutes or until golden brown. Cool 1 minute before removing to wire racks.

Nutrition information: per cookie: 100 calories, 6g fat (3g saturated fat), 20mg cholesterol, 77mg sodium, 11g carbohydrate (7g sugars, 0 fiber), 1g protein.

55. Sweet Potato Soufflé

Sweet Potato Soufflé is a classic dessert made up of mashed sweet potatoes, sugar, butter, eggs and milk. It has a wonderful texture - a creamy interior and a soft, light, fluffy top. It's the perfect end to a holiday meal.
Serving: 8
Preparation Time: 15 minutes
Ready Time: 40 minutes

Ingredients:
2 pounds sweet potatoes, 2 tablespoons melted butter, 3/4 cup white sugar, 2 eggs, 1/2 cup milk, 1 teaspoon nutmeg, 1/4 teaspoon ground cloves

Instructions:
1. Preheat oven to 350 degrees F (175 degrees C). Lightly grease an 8-inch square baking dish.
2. Cook sweet potatoes in boiling water for 20 minutes or until tender; drain. Mash sweet potatoes and mix in melted butter and sugar. Beat in eggs, milk, nutmeg and cloves until smooth. Transfer to prepared baking dish.
3. Bake for 25 to 30 minutes in preheated oven, or until top is golden brown.

Nutrition information: Calories per serving: 224; Total Fat: 7.3g, Sodium: 110mg; Total Carbs: 36.4g; Sugars: 21.3g; Protein: 3g; Fiber: 2.7g.

56. Southern Cornbread Pudding

Southern Cornbread Pudding is a classic, soul-satisfying sweet dish that's easy to make. The sweet pudding is made of moist, crumbly cornbread, dabbed with butter, and combined with a simple custard mixture.
Serving: 8
Preparation time: 10 minutes
Ready time: 45 minutes

Ingredients:
- 1/2 cup butter
- 2 cups crumbled cornbread
- 2 cups whole milk
- 1/2 cup white sugar
- 2 eggs
- 1/2 teaspoon ground cinnamon
- 1/4 teaspoon ground nutmeg

Instructions:
1. Preheat oven to 350 degrees F (175 degrees C). Grease a 8-inch baking dish with butter.
2. Place the cornbread crumbles into a medium bowl, and set aside.
3. In a separate bowl, whisk together the eggs, milk, sugar, nutmeg, and cinnamon until well blended.
4. Pour the egg mixture over the cornbread, and fold gently to combine. Allow the mixture to sit for 5 minutes.
5. Pour the batter into the prepared baking dish. Dot the top with butter, and bake for 40 minutes, or until set.

Nutrition information:
Calories: 215; Protein: 5g; Fat: 10g; Sodium: 119mg; Carbohydrates: 25g; Sugar: 14g; Fiber: 2g.

57. Pimento Cheese Dip

Pimento Cheese Dip is an indulgent and creamy dip that is perfect for enjoying with chips or vegetables. It is a classic southern United States appetizer perfect for any special occasion.
Serving: 6
Preparation Time: 10 minutes

Ready Time: 30 minutes

Ingredients:
- 8 ounces sharp cheddar cheese, grated
- 4 ounces cream cheese, softened
- ½ cup mayonnaise
- 2 tablespoons diced jarred pimentos
- 2 tablespoons diced scallions
- ½ teaspoon Worcestershire sauce
- ¼ teaspoon garlic powder
- Dash of hot sauce

Instructions:
1. In a medium bowl, combine the cheese, cream cheese, mayonnaise, pimentos, scallions, Worcestershire sauce, garlic powder, and hot sauce.
2. Mix together until everything is fully combined.
3. Transfer the dip to a small baking dish or serving bowl.
4. Bake at 350°F for 25-30 minutes, or until the dip is bubbly and golden.
5. Let the dip cool for about 5 minutes before serving with chips or vegetables.

Nutrition information:
Calories: 224, Fat: 18g, Saturated Fat: 8g, Carbohydrates: 3g, Protein: 11g, Cholesterol: 42mg, Sodium: 323mg, Fiber: 0g, Sugar: 1g.

58. Chocolate Pecan Pie Bars

Chocolate Pecan Pie Bars are a delicious and easy-to-make dessert which combine rich chocolate flavors with the nuttiness of pecans.
Serving: Makes 16 bars
Preparation time: 10 minutes
Ready time: 40 minutes

Ingredients:
- 1 cup butter, melted
- 2 ½ cups graham cracker cookie crumbs
- 2 cups confectioners' sugar
- 1 cup pecans, chopped

- ½ cup semi-sweet chocolate chips, melted
- 1 teaspoon vanilla extract
- 1 tablespoon Kahlua (optional)

Instructions:
1. Preheat oven to 350°F. Grease a 9x13-inch baking dish.
2. In a medium bowl, combine melted butter, graham cracker cookie crumbs, confectioners' sugar, pecans, melted semi-sweet chocolate chips, vanilla extract and Kahlua (if using).
3. Mix together until just combined.
4. Spread into prepared baking dish and press firmly into an even layer.
5. Bake for 35-40 minutes, until the edges are lightly golden brown. Remove from oven and cool completely before cutting into 16 bars.

Nutrition information: Per serving: Calories 364, Fat 21 g, Saturated fat 10 g, Cholesterol 37 mg, Sodium 116 mg, Carbohydrates 41 g, Fiber 1 g, Protein 3 g, Sugar 28 g.

59. Peach Pound Cake

A classic Southern dessert, Peach Pound Cake is a soft and tender treat that melts in your mouth. With sweet peaches and a creamy, buttery cake base, this recipe is sure to be loved by everyone.
Serving: 8-10
Preparation Time: 10 minutes
Ready Time: 1 hour

Ingredients:
- 1 cup (2 sticks) butter, softened
- 3 cups granulated sugar
- 5 eggs
- 3 cups all-purpose flour
- 2 teaspoons baking powder
- 1/2 teaspoon salt
- 3/4 cup whole milk
- 2 cups diced fresh or canned peaches
- 1 teaspoon vanilla extract

Instructions:
1. Preheat oven to 350 degrees F (175 degrees C). Grease and flour a 10-inch tube or bundt pan.
2. In a large bowl, cream together butter and sugar until light and fluffy. Beat in eggs one at a time, mixing well after each addition.
3. In a separate bowl, sift together flour, baking powder, and salt. Gradually add to butter mixture, alternating with milk. Beat in vanilla extract, then fold in peaches.
4. Pour into prepared pan and bake for 50-60 minutes, or until a toothpick inserted into the center of the cake comes out clean.
5. Allow to cool before serving.

Nutrition information: Per Serving: 780 calories; 24.3 g fat; 135 mg cholesterol; 490 mg sodium; 133.2 g carbohydrates; 6.2 g protein.

60. Fried Okra

Fried okra is a southern favorite made with fresh okra dipped in a cornmeal batter and fried until crispy and golden.
Serving: 4
Preparation Time: 10 minutes
Ready Time: 10 minutes

Ingredients:
-2 cups fresh okra, cut into slices
-1 teaspoon salt
-1/2 cup cornmeal
-1/2 cup all-purpose flour
-Vegetable oil, for frying

Instructions:
1. In a large bowl, toss the okra with the salt.
2. In a separate bowl, mix together the cornmeal and flour.
3. Heat vegetable oil in a large skillet over medium-high heat.
4. Dip the okra slices in the cornmeal batter, coating both sides thoroughly.
5. Gently place the battered okra in the hot oil and fry for about 3 minutes per side, or until golden brown and crispy.

6. Remove the okra from the oil and set on a paper towel-lined plate to cool and drain off excess oil.

Nutrition information: Calories: 150, Total Fat: 7g, Cholesterol: 0mg, Sodium: 380mg, Total Carbohydrate: 18g, Dietary Fiber: 3g, Protein: 4g.

61. Blackberry Jam Cake

This delicious Blackberry Jam Cake has a delightful combination of tender crumb cake and sweet jam with a hint of almond flavor. It makes a perfect tea-time treat or an indulgent afternoon snack.
Serving: 8
Preparation Time: 15 minutes
Ready Time: 45 minutes

Ingredients:
- 1 cup almond flour
- ½ cup all-purpose flour
- ½ teaspoon baking powder
- ½ teaspoon baking soda
- ¼ teaspoon salt
- 6 tablespoons unsalted butter, softened
- ½ cup granulated sugar
- 2 large eggs
- ½ teaspoon almond extract
- ½ cup buttermilk
- ¾ cup blackberry jam

Instructions:
1. Preheat oven to 350° F. Grease an 8-inch round baking pan and set aside.
2. In a large bowl, whisk together almond flour, all-purpose flour, baking powder, baking soda, and salt. Set aside.
3. In a separate bowl, cream together butter and sugar. Add the eggs and almond extract and mix until combined.
4. Alternate adding dry Ingredients and buttermilk to the wet Ingredients, mixing after each addition until just combined.

5. Spread batter evenly into the prepared pan. Drop spoonfuls of blackberry jam over the top of the batter and swirled it around with a knife.
6. Bake for 40 to 45 minutes, or until a knife inserted in the center comes out clean.
7. Cool in the pan before serving.

Nutrition information: cal 84, fat 4.8g, sat fat 2.8g, chol 17mg, sodium 83.7mg, carbs 10.2g, fiber 0.4g, sugar 6.4g, protein 1.7g

62. Sausage and Grits Casserole

Sausage and Grits Casserole is an easy, flavorful Southern comfort food dish that the entire family will love!
Serving: Serves 4
Preparation time: 10 minutes
Ready time: 30 minutes

Ingredients:
-1 pound pork sausage
-2 cups cooked grits
-1 1/2 cups shredded cheddar cheese
-2 cups milk
-3 eggs
-1/2 teaspoon garlic powder
-Salt and pepper to taste
-1/4 cup butter

Instructions:
1. Preheat your oven to 375 degrees.
2. In a skillet over medium heat, cook the sausage until it is browned and cooked through. Drain any excess grease.
3. In a large bowl, combine cooked grits, cheddar cheese, milk, eggs, garlic powder, salt, and pepper until well blended.
4. Spread the sausage in an even layer into the bottom of a 9x13 baking dish.
5. Pour the grits mixture over top of the sausage.
6. Dot the top of the casserole with butter.

7. Bake in preheated oven for 30 minutes or until the grits are set and golden brown.

Nutrition information: Per Serving: 600 calories, 37g fat, 22g carbohydrates, 33g protein

63. Caramel Apple Upside-Down Cake

Caramel Apple Upside-Down Cake is an easy mix of apples, caramel, and cake mix that creates a decadent, deliciously sweet upside-down cake.
Serving: Makes one 9x13 inch cake
Preparation time: 20 minutes
Ready time:1 hour 5 minutes

Ingredients:
-3 cups diced Granny Smith apples (about 2 large apples)
-1/4 cup unsalted butter
-1 cup light brown sugar
-2 tablespoons corn syrup
-1 18-ounce box yellow cake mix
-1/3 cup granulated sugar
-3/4 cup vegetable oil
-3 large eggs
-2 teaspoons ground cinnamon
-1/2 teaspoon nutmeg

Instructions:
1. Preheat oven to 350°F (180°C). Grease a 9x13 inch baking pan and set aside.
2. In a medium-sized saucepan, melt the butter over medium heat. Stir in the brown sugar and corn syrup, and bring to a boil.
3. Remove from heat and pour into the bottom of the prepared pan. Arrange diced apples over the caramel.
4. Whisk together cake mix, granulated sugar, oil, eggs, cinnamon, and nutmeg in a large bowl until blended. Scrape the batter into the pan, spreading evenly.

5. Bake the cake for 40 to 45 minutes, or until a cake tester inserted into the center comes out clean. Cool for 10 minutes before inverting onto a plate. Serve warm or at room temperature.

Nutrition information: Servings 12, Calories 200, Fat 7.3 g, Carbohydrate 33.3 g, Protein 2.2 g, Sodium 78 mg.

64. Bourbon Bread Pudding

Bourbon Bread Pudding is a delicious dessert that combines tender bread cubes, crunchy caramelized sugar, and liquid infusion of creamy bourbon. This classic dessert is an easy yet impressive way to end a dinner party.
Serving: Serves 8
Preparation Time: 10 minutes
Ready Time: 45 minutes

Ingredients:
- 3 cups of cubed white bread
- 2 large eggs
- 3/4 cup of white sugar
- 2 cups of whole milk
- 2 tablespoons of bourbon
- 2 tablespoons of melted butter
- 1/2 teaspoon of cinnamon
- 1/2 teaspoon of nutmeg
- 1/4 teaspoon of vanilla extract
- Pinch of salt

Instructions:
1. Preheat oven to 350°F. Spread the cubes of bread onto a baking sheet. Toast in the oven for about 10 minutes or until lightly toasted.
2. In a large bowl, beat together the eggs and sugar until smooth.
3. In a separate bowl, combine the milk, bourbon, butter, cinnamon, nutmeg, vanilla extract, and salt.
4. Add the toasted bread cubes to the bowl with the egg and sugar mixture and mix to combine.
5. Pour the liquid mixture over the bread and stir to combine.

6. Grease an 8x8 inch baking dish with butter. Pour the bread pudding mixture into the dish and spread evenly.
7. Place the dish in the preheated oven and bake for about 45 minutes or until golden brown.
8. Allow the bread pudding to cool slightly before serving.

Nutrition information: Serving size: 1/8 of recipe, Calories: 220, Total Fat: 8g, Saturated Fat: 5g, Cholesterol: 65mg, Sodium: 160mg, Total Carbohydrate: 29g, Dietary Fiber: 1g, Total Sugars: 16g, Protein: 6g.

65. Apple Cider Doughnuts

Apple Cider Doughnuts are a delicious, sweet treat that are easy to make and full of warm autumn flavors.
Serving: Makes 8-10 Doughnuts
Preparation Time: 25 minutes
Ready Time: 1 hour & 10 minutes

Ingredients:
-2 cups all-purpose flour
-2 teaspoons baking powder
-1/4 teaspoon nutmeg
-1/2 teaspoon cinnamon
-1/4 teaspoon cloves
-1/2 teaspoon salt
-1 large egg, beaten
-1/2 cup granulated sugar
-1/2 cup apple cider
-1/4 cup vegetable or canola oil
-Extra granulated sugar for coating

Instructions:
1. Preheat oven to 350 °F (177 °C). Grease doughnut pan.
2. In a large bowl, whisk together the flour, baking powder, nutmeg, cinnamon, cloves, and salt.
3. In a medium bowl, whisk together the egg, sugar, apple cider, and oil.

4. Pour the wet Ingredients into the dry Ingredients and mix until just combined.
5. Spoon the batter into the prepared pan, filling each about 3/4 of the way full.
6. Bake for 10-12 minutes, until golden brown. Let cool for about 5 minutes.
7. Gently remove the doughnuts from the pan with the help of a butter knife and roll in extra sugar.

Nutrition information:
Serving size: 1 Doughnut
Calories: 169 Total Fat: 4g Carbohydrates: 29g Protein: 2g

66. Sweet Potato Cinnamon Rolls

Enjoy these homemade sweet potato cinnamon rolls that are rolled with potato puree and brown sugar cinnamon filling. These warm and fragrant treats are sure to please friends and family! Serving: 10-12 rolls Preparation time: 20 minutes Ready time: 1 hour

Ingredients:
- 2 cups mashed sweet potato
- 2 1/2 teaspoons active dry yeast
- 2/3 cup warm water
- 1 cup warm milk
- 4 cups all-purpose flour
- 1 teaspoon salt
- 4 tablespoons light brown sugar
- 2 tablespoons softened butter
- 2 teaspoons ground cinnamon

Instructions:
1. In a small bowl, dissolve the yeast in the warm water and let it sit until it is foamy, about 5 minutes.
2. In a large bowl, combine the mashed sweet potato, warm milk, all-purpose flour, and salt. Mix until the dough comes together.
3. On a lightly floured surface, knead the dough for 8-10 minutes.

4. Place the dough in a lightly greased bowl and cover with a damp cloth. Let it rise until it is doubled in size, about 1 hour.
5. On a lightly floured surface, roll out the dough into a 16x10-inch rectangle.
6. In a small bowl, combine the light brown sugar, softened butter and cinnamon. Mix until combined.
7. Spread the mixture over the dough. Roll the dough into a log and cut into 1-inch pieces.
8. Place the rolls in a lightly greased 13x9-inch baking pan. Cover and let the rolls rise until they are doubled in size, about another hour.
9. Preheat the oven to 375 degrees F (190 degrees C).
10. Bake for 20-25 minutes, or until the rolls are lightly golden brown.
11. Let the rolls cool for 10 minutes before serving.

Nutrition information: Serving size: 1 roll, Calories: 200, Total Fat: 5 g, Saturated Fat: 3 g, Cholesterol: 10 mg, Sodium: 220 mg, Total Carbohydrate: 33 g, Dietary Fiber: 2 g, Sugars: 8 g, Protein: 5 g.

67. Peanut Butter Pie

Peanut Butter Pie is a delicious dessert that combines the creamy and sweet flavor of peanut butter with a flaky crust. It is a popular favorite for dinner parties and special occasions.
Serving: Makes one (1) 9-inch pie, serves 8
Preparation Time: 20 minutes
Ready Time: 1 hour

Ingredients:
- 9 inch ready-made graham cracker, chocolate, or vanilla crust
- 2/3 cup creamy peanut butter
- 2 cups heavy cream
- 1/2 cup powdered sugar
- 1 teaspoon vanilla extract
- 1/2 teaspoon salt

Instructions:
1. Preheat oven to 350°F.
2. Spread peanut butter in the pre-baked crust.

3. In a medium bowl, whisk together the heavy cream, powdered sugar, vanilla extract, and salt.
4. Using an electric mixer on medium-high speed, beat the cream mixture until it holds stiff peaks.
5. Spread the cream mixture over the peanut butter layer and spread into an even layer.
6. Bake for 25 minutes. Set aside to cool for 10 minutes, then place in the fridge for 1 hour to set.

Nutrition information: (per slice) Calories: 459, Fat: 27g, Saturated fat: 8g, Sodium: 334mg, Carbs: 47g, Sugar: 17g, Protein: 8g

68. Bacon Cheddar Cornbread

This Bacon Cheddar Cornbread is a savory and delicious combination of a classic Southern side dish. With crispy bacon, melted cheddar cheese, and flavorful cornbread, it's a great addition to any meal.
Serving: 8
Preparation Time: 10 minutes
Ready Time: 40 minutes

Ingredients:
-1 cup all-purpose flour
-1 cup yellow cornmeal
-2 teaspoons baking powder
-1 teaspoon kosher salt
-1/3 cup melted butter
-2 large eggs
-1 cup of half and half milk
-1 cup of cooked and crumbled bacon
-1 cup of shredded cheddar cheese

Instructions:
1. Preheat oven to 375F. Grease an 8-inch square baking dish with cooking spray.
2. In a medium bowl, whisk together the flour, cornmeal, baking powder and salt.
3. In a separate bowl, whisk together the butter, eggs and half and half.

4. Pour the wet Ingredients into the dry Ingredients and mix until just combined.
5. Pour the batter into the greased baking dish and sprinkle the bacon and cheddar cheese over the top.
6. Bake for 30-40 minutes or until a toothpick inserted into the center comes out clean.
7. Let the cornbread cool for 5 minutes before serving.

Nutrition information: Calories: 297; Fat: 15 g; Saturated fat: 9 g; Carbohydrates: 28 g; Sodium: 620 mg; Fiber: 1 g; Protein: 12 g.

69. Lemon Blueberry Bundt Cake

Lemon Blueberry Bundt Cake is a delectable cake made with butter, fresh lemons, and juicy blueberries. Serve it fresh from the oven with a dollop of cream or lemon curd on the side for a delightful treat.
Serving: 8
Preparation time: 15 minutes
Ready time: 65 minutes

Ingredients:
- 2 cups all purpose flour
- 1 teaspoon baking powder
- 1/4 teaspoon baking soda
- 1/2 teaspoon salt
- 3/4 cup (1 1/2 sticks) butter, softened
- 2 cups granulated sugar
- 4 large eggs
- 1 teaspoon vanilla extract
- Zest of 1 lemon
- 3/4 cup sour cream
- 2 cups fresh blueberries

Instructions:
1. Preheat oven to 350 degrees F. Grease and flour a 10-cup bundt pan.
2. Sift together the flour, baking powder, baking soda, and salt; set aside.

3. In a large bowl, cream together the butter and sugar with an electric mixer. Beat in the eggs one at a time, then stir in the vanilla and lemon zest.
4. Add the flour mixture alternately with the sour cream, stirring just until blended. Gently stir in the blueberries.
5. Transfer to the prepared pan and bake 55 to 65 minutes, or until a toothpick inserted into the center comes out clean. Cool in the pan for 10 minutes before turning out onto a rack to cool completely.

Nutrition information: Per serving (1/8 of cake): 200 calories, 9 g fat, 3 g saturated fat, 34 g carbohydrates, 1 g dietary fiber, 24 g sugar, 3 g protein.

70. Mississippi Mud Brownies

Rich and intensely chocolate, Mississippi Mud Brownies are a decadent dessert that will make everyone's mouth water. This recipe is sure to be a crowd pleaser!
Serving: 9
Preparation Time: 20 minutes
Ready Time: 1 hour

Ingredients:
- ½ cup butter
- 1 ¼ cup granulated sugar
- 2 eggs
- 2 teaspoons vanilla
- 1 cup all-purpose flour
- ¾ cup cocoa powder
- ¼ teaspoon baking powder
- ¼ teaspoon salt
- 1 cup semi-sweet chocolate chips
- 1 cup mini marshmallows
- 2 tablespoons butter

Instructions:
1. Preheat oven to 350°F and grease a 9x9 inch baking dish.

2. In a medium bowl, combine flour, cocoa powder, baking powder, and salt.
3. In a separate bowl, cream together butter and sugar. Beat in eggs one at a time, then add the vanilla.
4. Gradually add the dry Ingredients to the wet Ingredients, stirring until fully combined.
5. Spread the batter evenly into the prepared baking dish.
6. Sprinkle the chocolate chips and marshmallows over the top of the brownies.
7. Dot the dough with the remaining 2 tablespoons of butter and bake for 25 minutes, or until a toothpick inserted into the center comes out clean.
8. Let the brownies cool completely before cutting into 9 squares.

Nutrition information: Per serving - Calories: 265; Carbs: 32g; Protein: 2g; Fat: 15g; Sodium: 140mg.

71. Baked Collard Greens

Baked Collard Greens are a savory and hearty side dish that is perfect for special occasions. The collard greens are cooked within a baking dish with simple Ingredients, such as olive oil and garlic, that enhance the flavor.
Serving: Serves 8
Preparation Time: 10 minutes
Ready Time: 45 minutes

Ingredients:
-1/4 cup olive oil
-8 cloves garlic, minced
-6 bunches collard greens, washed, stems removed, and roughly chopped
-1 teaspoon smoked paprika
-1 teaspoon sea salt
-1/4 teaspoon ground black pepper

Instructions:
1. Preheat oven to 350 degrees F (175 degrees C).
2. In a large oven-safe dish, combine olive oil and garlic.

3. Add collard greens and mix until evenly combined.
4. Sprinkle smoked paprika, sea salt, and pepper over the greens.
5. Cover the dish with aluminum foil and bake for 30 minutes.
6. Remove foil and bake for an additional 15 minutes.

Nutrition information:
Per Serving: 117 calories; 6.2 g fat; 12.7 g carbohydrates; 2.9 g protein; 7 mg cholesterol; 297 mg sodium.

72. Southern-Style Banana Pudding Cheesecake

Southern-style banana pudding cheesecake is the perfect combination of banana pudding and cheesecake, giving you the perfect creamy, fruity mix in a dessert.
Serving: 8
Preparation time: 30 minutes
Ready time: 2 hours

Ingredients:
- 2 pre-made 9-inch graham cracker pie crusts
- 1 8-ounce block of cream cheese
- 1 14-ounce can of sweetened condensed milk
- 1 large banana, mashed
- ⅓ cup of white sugar
- 2 tablespoons of cornstarch
- 1 teaspoon of lemon juice
- 1 teaspoon of macaroon extract
- 2 egg yolks
- 2 tablespoons of butter, melted

Instructions:
1. Preheat oven to 350°F.
2. In a medium bowl, whisk cream cheese until smooth.
3. Add condensed milk, mashed banana, sugar, cornstarch, lemon juice, and macaroon extract.
4. Add egg yolks and whisk until smooth.
5. Divide the mixture between the two graham cracker pie crusts.

6. Bake for 25-30 minutes, or until the edges are golden brown and the center is set.
7. Allow the cheesecakes to cool before serving.

Nutrition information: Per serving, this banana pudding cheesecake has 420 calories, 17g fat, 56g carbohydrates, and 7g protein.

73. Buttermilk Fried Pork Chops

Buttermilk Fried Pork Chops are an incredibly delicious and savory dish. The buttermilk creates a nice crunchy coating when cooked. This will become a family favorite for sure!
Serving: 5-6
Preparation Time: 25 minutes
Ready Time: 35 minutes

Ingredients:
- 12 pork chops
- 1¼ cups buttermilk
- 1 teaspoon garlic powder
- 2 tablespoons vegetable oil
- 2 teaspoons paprika
- 1 teaspoon salt
- ½ teaspoon black pepper
- 1 cup all-purpose flour
- 2 tablespoons butter

Instructions:
1. Place the pork chops in a shallow dish and pour in the buttermilk. Sprinkle in garlic powder and stir to combine. Cover and place the pork chops in the refrigerator for at least 30 minutes.
2. In a shallow dish, combine the vegetable oil, paprika, salt, and pepper.
3. Place the flour and butter in separate shallow dishes.
4. Preheat the oven to 350 degrees F (175 degrees C).
5. Remove the pork chops from the buttermilk and dredge each one in the flour. Then dip into the butter mixture and then into the oil mixture. Place the coated pork chops onto a baking sheet.

6. Bake on the middle oven shelf for 25 minutes.

Nutrition information:
- Amount per serving (5-6)
- Calories: 745
- Total Fat: 33.4g
- Saturated Fat: 11.7g
- Cholesterol: 177mg
- Sodium: 638mg
- Total Carbohydrates: 58.2g
- Dietary Fiber: 1.7g
- Sugars: 0.3g
- Protein: 50.5g

74. Pecan Sandies

Pecan Sandies are buttery cookie packed with crunchy pecans and a dusting of sugar. Perfect to nibble on, these cookies are an easy and delicious treat for kids and adults alike.
Serving: Makes about 2 dozen cookies
Preparation Time: 10 minutes
Ready Time: 20 minutes

Ingredients:
2 cups all-purpose flour
1 cup butter, softened
1/2 cup packed light brown sugar
1/3 cup chopped pecans, lightly toasted
1/2 teaspoon salt
1 teaspoon pure vanilla extract

Instructions:
1. Preheat oven to 350 degrees F.
2. In a large bowl, cream together butter and brown sugar until light and fluffy.
3. Add flour, salt, vanilla extract, and toasted pecans, and mix until the mixture forms a soft dough.

4. Shape the dough into 1-inch balls and place on an ungreased baking sheet.
5. Bake for 10-12 minutes, until cookies are lightly browned.
6. Allow cookies to cool on the baking sheet for 2 minutes before transferring to a cooling rack to cool completely.

Nutrition information: Serving Size: 1 cookie, Calories: 118, Total Fat: 7g, Saturated Fat: 4g, Cholesterol: 15mg, Sodium: 71mg, Total Carbohydrate: 13g, Dietary Fiber: 1g, Sugars: 6g, Protein: 1g.

75. Pumpkin Bread

This delicious, easy-to-bake pumpkin bread is filled with fall flavors like cinnamon, nutmeg, and allspice. Perfect for your chilly season celebrations!
Serving: 12 slices
Preparation time: 10 minutes
Ready time: 1 hour

Ingredients:
- 2 cups all-purpose flour
- 2 teaspoons baking powder
- ½ teaspoon baking soda
- 1 teaspoon ground cinnamon
- ½ teaspoon ground nutmeg
- ¼ teaspoon ground allspice
- ½ teaspoon salt
- ½ cup (1 stick) butter, softened
- 1 cup sugar
- 2 eggs
- 1 cup canned pumpkin puree
- ½ cup chopped walnuts (optional)

Instructions:
1. Preheat your oven to 350°F (175°C). Grease and flour a 9x5-inch loaf pan.
2. In a medium mixing bowl, combine the flour with baking powder, baking soda, cinnamon, nutmeg, allspice, and salt; set aside.

3. In a separate bowl, cream together the softened butter and sugar until light and fluffy. Beat in the eggs one at a time. Stir in the pumpkin puree until well blended.
4. Gradually add the dry Ingredients to the pumpkin mixture and mix until just combined. Stir in the chopped nuts if desired.
5. Pour the batter into the prepared pan and bake for 1 hour, or until a toothpick inserted into the center comes out clean.

Nutrition information: Per slice of Pumpkin Bread contains 240 calories, 11g fat, 31g carbohydrates and 5g protein.

76. Honey Butter Biscuits

Honey Butter Biscuits are light, fluffy, and full of flavor. These biscuits are easy and quick to prepare. Serve them with butter, jam, or honey butter, or pair them with a savory dish.
Serving: 8-10 biscuits
Preparation Time: 10 minutes
Ready Time: 20 minutes

Ingredients:
2 cups all-purpose flour
2 teaspoons baking powder
1 teaspoon baking soda
¼ teaspoon salt
1 teaspoon granulated sugar
4 tablespoons cold unsalted butter, cut into cubes
¾ cup buttermilk
¼ cup honey

Instructions:
1. Preheat the oven to 400°F (204°C).
2. In a medium bowl, whisk together the flour, baking powder, baking soda, salt, and sugar.
3. Cut in the butter using a pastry blender or two forks until the mixture resembles coarse crumbs.
4. In a small bowl, mix together the buttermilk and honey.

5. Add the buttermilk mixture to the flour mixture and stir until just combined.
6. Turn the dough out onto a lightly floured surface and knead gently for 1-2 minutes.
7. Roll the dough out to ½-inch thickness and use a biscuit cutter (or a glass) to cut out circles.
8. Place the biscuits on an ungreased baking sheet and bake for 15-20 minutes, or until lightly browned.

Nutrition information: 182 calories, 8 g fat, 24 g carbohydrates, 2 g protein, 1 g fiber, 106 mg sodium.

77. Southern Peach Tea

Southern Peach Tea is an easy and delicious beverage for hot summer days. It is a simple drink made with sweet tea, fresh or frozen peaches, and a few more Ingredients that come together for an amazing iced tea experience.
Serving: 4-5
Preparation Time: 10 minutes
Ready Time: 10 minutes

Ingredients:
- 6 cups of water
- 2 black tea bags
- 1/2 cup granulated sugar
- 2 cups fresh or frozen peaches, pitted and chopped into small pieces
- 2 tablespoons peach syrup
- 2 tablespoons fresh lemon juice

Instructions:
1. Bring 6 cups of water to a boil in a large pot. Once boiling, add tea bags and steep for 4 minutes.
2. Turn off heat and add sugar, stirring until sugar is completely dissolved.
3. Once boiling is returned, add peaches, peach syrup, and lemon juice, and simmer for 5 minutes.

4. Remove from heat and strain liquid through a fine mesh sieve, pushing on the peaches to extract as much liquid as possible.
5. Let tea cool completely before serving over ice.

Nutrition information: Per serving (approx. 1 cup): Calories: 86, Total Fat 0g, Saturated Fat 0g, Cholesterol 0mg, Sodium 0mg, Carbohydrates 22g, Fiber 0g, Sugar 21g, Protein 0g.

78. Chocolate Fudge Cake

This Chocolate Fudge Cake is an irresistible treat perfect for any special occasion. It is deliciously moist and topped with a rich, buttery fudge frosting.
Serving: 8-10
Preparation Time: 45 minutes
Ready Time: 1 hour 35 minutes

Ingredients:
- 1 & 1/4 cups all-purpose flour
- 1/4 cup cocoa powder
- 3/4 teaspoon baking soda
- 1/2 teaspoon baking powder
- 1/2 teaspoon salt
- 1/2 cup (1 stick) butter, softened
- 1 cup packed light brown sugar
- 2 large eggs
- 1 teaspoon pure vanilla extract
- 3/4 cup full fat Greek yogurt
- 1/3 cup semi-sweet chocolate chips, divided

Instructions:
1. Preheat oven to 350°F (180°C). Grease an 8" cake pan and line with parchment paper.
2. In a mixing bowl, whisk together flour, cocoa powder, baking soda, baking powder and salt.
3. In the bowl of a stand mixer using the paddle attachment, beat the butter and brown sugar until fluffy, about 3 minutes. Add eggs, one at a time, then add the vanilla and yogurt.

4. With mixer on low speed, add the dry Ingredients and mix until just combined.
5. Fold in 1/4 cup of the chocolate chips.
6. Spread the batter evenly into the prepared pan. Sprinkle remaining chocolate chips over the top.
7. Bake for 25-30 minutes, or until a toothpick inserted in centre comes out clean. Allow to cool on a wire rack.

Nutrition information: Serving size: 1 slice, Calories: 314, Total Fat: 15 g, Saturated Fat: 9 g, Trans Fat: 0 g, Cholesterol: 59 mg, Sodium: 218 mg, Carbohydrates: 42 g, Fiber: 2 g, Sugar: 24 g, Protein: 4 g

79. Buttermilk Panna Cotta

Buttermilk Panna Cotta is a delicious and elegant Italian dessert that is sweet, creamy, and subtly tangy.
Serving: 8
Preparation time: 20 minutes
Ready time: 6 hours

Ingredients:
- 2 cups heavy cream
- 1/2 cup Buttermilk
- 1/4 cup granulated sugar
- 1/4 teaspoon pure vanilla extract
- 1 packet (2 teaspoons) gelatin
- 2 tablespoons cold water

Instructions:
1. In a medium saucepan, combine the heavy cream, buttermilk, sugar and vanilla over medium heat. Bring to a low simmer and stire until sugar has dissolved.
2. Meanwhile, in a small bowl, sprinkle the gelatin over the cold water and allow to sit for 5 minutes, to soften.
3. Add softened gelatin to the warm cream mixture and stir until dissolved.

4. Remove from heat and pour into 8 individual 4-ounce molds, or a single 8x8-inch baking dish.
5. Refrigerate for at least 6 hours before serving.

Nutrition information: Calories: 175 | Fat: 12 g | Carbs: 10 g | Protein: 4 g

80. Sweet Potato Pancakes

Sweet Potato Pancakes are the perfect breakfast food. They are filled with protein and vitamins and are sure to energize your day. Serve them with a dollop of maple syrup or peanut butter or enjoy them on their own for a delicious treat.
Serving: Makes 8 pancakes
Preparation time: 10 minutes
Ready time: 25 minutes

Ingredients:
- 1 large sweet potato, peeled and grated
- 1 cup all-purpose flour
- 2 tablespoons granulated sugar
- 2 teaspoons baking powder
- ½ teaspoon ground cinnamon
- ¼ teaspoon sea salt
- 2 large eggs
- ¼ cup whole milk
- 2 tablespoons melted butter

Instructions:
1. In a large bowl, combine the grated sweet potato, flour, sugar, baking powder, cinnamon, and salt.
2. In a separate bowl, whisk together the eggs, milk, and melted butter.
3. Pour the wet Ingredients into the dry Ingredients and mix until just combined.
4. Heat a large skillet over medium heat. Add a teaspoon of oil and let it heat until shimmering.
5. Using an ice cream scoop or a ¼ cup measure, drop batter onto the hot skillet.

6. Cook for 3-4 minutes, or until the edges are golden brown.
7. Flip the pancakes over and cook on the other side for an additional 2-3 minutes.
8. Remove the pancakes from the pan and set aside.
9. Continue cooking the remaining pancakes, adding more oil to the pan as needed.

Nutrition information:
Serving size: 1 pancake
Calories: 105 kcal
Fat: 4.5g
Carbohydrates: 14.5g
Protein: 3g

81. Strawberry Swirl Pound Cake

Experience the delicious and moist flavor of this Strawberry Swirl Pound Cake! This decadent dessert is a fun spin on a classic pound cake recipe and would make an ideal addition to any gathering.
Serving: 8
Preparation Time: 20 minutes
Ready Time: 1 hour and 10 minutes

Ingredients:
- 4 large eggs
- 2 cups granulated sugar
- 1 cup butter, melted
- 2 teaspoons real vanilla extract
- 3 cups all-purpose flour
- 1/2 teaspoon baking powder
- 1/4 teaspoon salt
- 1/4 cup whole milk
- 1/4 cup strawberry jam

Instructions:
1. Preheat the oven to 350°F and prepare a 9-inch center tube pan by greasing the sides and bottom.

2. In a large bowl, mix together the eggs, sugar, butter, and vanilla extract.
3. In a separate bowl, sift the flour, baking powder, and salt. Gradually add the dry Ingredients to the wet Ingredients and mix until fully combined. Stir in the whole milk.
4. Pour the batter into the prepared tube pan. Swirl the strawberry jam into the batter using a knife.
5. Bake in preheated oven for about 50-60 minutes, or until golden brown and a toothpick inserted into the center of the cake comes out clean.
6. Let cool completely before serving.

Nutrition information: Serving Size - 1/8 cake, Amount Per Serving - Calories 333, Total Fat 14.7g, Sodium 211.9mg, Total Carbohydrates 47.1g, Sugars 27.5g, Protein 4.9g.

82. Southern-Style Grits

Southern-Style Grits are a creamy, savory dish with a classic southern flavor. It can be enjoyed morning, noon, or night.
Serving: 4
Preparation Time: 10 minutes
Ready Time: 20 minutes

Ingredients:
- 2 cups water
- ½ teaspoon salt
- 1 cup medium-grind grits
- 2 tablespoons butter
- 1 cup grated sharp cheddar cheese
- 2 tablespoons chopped chives

Instructions:
1. Bring the water and salt to a boil in a medium saucepan. Slowly stir in the grits. Reduce the heat to a simmer and cook for 5 minutes, stirring often.

2. Once the grits are creamy and thick, add the butter, cheddar, and chives. Continue cooking for 15 minutes or until the cheese is melted, stirring often. Serve hot.

Nutrition information:
Serving size: 1 (4 ounce)
Calories: 312 Fat: 15.2 g Carbs: 32.7 g Protein: 10 g Sodium: 347 mg
Fiber: 1 g

83. Chocolate Chip Pecan Cookies

Delicious and chewy Chocolate Chip Pecan Cookies make a great treat to share with friends or family! Try adding in some other Ingredients like white chocolate chips or macadamia nuts to give them even more flavor.
Serving: Makes about 24 cookies
Preparation Time: 10 minutes
Ready Time: 20 minutes

Ingredients:
- 2 ½ cups all-purpose flour
- 1 teaspoon baking powder
- ½ teaspoon baking soda
- ½ teaspoon salt
- ¾ cup butter, melted
- ¾ cup packed light or dark brown sugar
- ½ cup granulated sugar
- 1 large egg
- 2 teaspoons vanilla extract
- 1 cup semi-sweet chocolate chips
- ½ cup chopped pecans

Instructions:
1. Preheat oven to 375 degrees F (190 degrees C).
2. In a medium bowl, mix together flour, baking powder, baking soda, and salt.
3. In a large bowl, beat together melted butter, brown sugar, and granulated sugar until blended. Beat in egg and vanilla extract.

4. Gradually blend in the dry Ingredients. Stir in chocolate chips and chopped pecans.
5. Drop dough by rounded spoonfuls onto ungreased cookie sheets.
6. Bake 8 to 10 minutes in the preheated oven, or until light and golden. Allow cookies to cool on baking sheet for 5 minutes before transferring to a wire rack to cool completely.

Nutrition information: Per serving (1 cookie): 191 calories; 9.3 g fat; 5.2 g saturated fat; 22.3 g carbohydrate; 2.1 g sugar; 2.3 g protein

84. Lemon Icebox Pie

Light, tart and creamy, this fresh lemon icebox pie is the perfect dessert to enjoy at any special occasion.
Serving: 8
Preparation time: 10 minutes
Ready time: 4 hours

Ingredients:
-1 ¾ cup graham cracker crumbs
-3 tablespoons sugar
-¼ cup melted butter
-1 can (14 oz.) sweetened condensed milk
-¾ cup fresh lemon juice
-2 tablespoons lemon zest
-¼ teaspoon salt
-2 cups heavy cream

Instructions:
1. Preheat oven to 350°F.
2. In a medium bowl, stir together graham cracker crumbs, sugar and melted butter until evenly combined.
3. Press into the bottom and up the sides of a 9-inch pie plate.
4. Bake for 8-10 minutes, or until golden-brown.
5. Remove from oven and let cool for 10 minutes.
6. In medium bowl, whisk together sweetened condensed milk, lemon juice, lemon zest and salt until thoroughly combined.
7. Pour filling into the cooled pie crust.

8. Refrigerate for at least 4 hours.
9. Just before serving, whip cream in a chilled bowl until soft peaks form.
10. Top pie with whipped cream.

Nutrition information: Per serving (1/8th of the pie): 386 calories; 24.3 g fat; 32.9 g carbs; 4.9 g protein

85. Cornbread Muffins

Cornbread muffins are the perfect accompaniment to any meal! Made with a combination of cornmeal, baking powder and buttermilk, these muffins are simple, moist, and slightly sweet.
Serving: Makes 12 muffins
Preparation time: 10 minutes
Ready time: 25 minutes

Ingredients:
- 1 cup all purpose flour
- 1 cup cornmeal
- 1 teaspoon baking powder
- 2 tablespoons sugar
- ½ teaspoon salt
- 1 cup buttermilk
- 1 egg
- 2 tablespoons melted butter

Instructions:
1. Preheat oven to 400° F (204° C). Grease a 12-cup muffin tin.
2. In a large bowl, combine flour, cornmeal, baking powder, sugar, and salt.
3. In a medium bowl, whisk together buttermilk, egg and melted butter.
4. Add wet Ingredients to the dry and stir until just combined.
5. Divide the batter evenly among the muffin cups.
6. Bake for 20-25 minutes, until muffins are golden and a toothpick inserted into the center comes out clean.
7. Let cool in the pan for 5 minutes, then remove to a wire rack to cool completely.

Nutrition information:
Serving size: 1 muffin
Calories per serving: 121
Total fat: 3.5 g
Total carbohydrates: 20 g
Total protein: 3 g

86. Bourbon Pecan Tart

Delicious and indulgent, this Bourbon Pecan Tart is sure to become a favorite. It features an oat- and pecan-based crust, a sweet and salty Bourbon-spiked filling, and a crown of roasted pecans.
Serving: 8
Preparation Time: 30 minutes
Ready Time: 2 hours

Ingredients:
- Crust:
- 2 1/4 cup rolled oats
- 2 1/4 cup toasted pecans
- 4 tablespoons sugar
- 5 tablespoons melted butter
- Filling:
- 1 cup packed light-brown sugar
- 3 large eggs
- 3 tablespoons Bourbon
- 1/4 teaspoon sea salt
- 3/4 cup melted butter
- Topping:
- 2 tablespoons Bourbon
- 2 tablespoons melted butter
- Salt to taste
- 2 cups toasted pecans

Instructions:
1. Preheat the oven to 350F.

2. Prepare the crust: In a food processor, pulse together the oats, pecans, and sugar. When the mixture looks like couscous, add the melted butter and pulse until the mixture is just combined.
3. Press the crust into a 9-inch tart pan or cake pan. Bake for 10 minutes.
4. Prepare the filling: In a large bowl, whisk together the brown sugar, eggs, Bourbon, and salt. Add the melted butter and mix until combined.
5. Pour the filling over the pre-baked crust and spread it evenly. Bake for 30 minutes, or until set.
6. Assemble the topping: In a small bowl, whisk together the Bourbon, melted butter, and salt.
7. Sprinkle the topping evenly over the tart and sprinkle with the toasted pecans. Bake for 30-35 more minutes, or until golden and set.
8. Let the tart cool in the pan for 10 minutes, then cut into slices and serve.

Nutrition information: (Per Serving) Calories: 528, Fat: 49g, Saturated fat: 18g, Cholesterol: 93mg, Sodium: 175mg, Protein: 7g, Carbohydrates: 22g, Sugar: 14g, Fiber: 4g

87. Fried Catfish

Fried Catfish is an American dish that is often served up on Friday's as a tasty alternative to fried fish. It can be served alone or with a variety of sides.
Serving: 4
Preparation Time: 10 minutes
Ready Time: 20 minutes

Ingredients:
-1 pound catfish fillets
-1 teaspoon garlic powder
-1 teaspoon paprika
-1 teaspoon salt
-1 teaspoon black pepper
-1/2 cup all-purpose flour
-2 tablespoons olive oil
-2 tablespoons butter

Instructions:
1. Preheat oven to 400 degrees Fahrenheit.
2. In a shallow bowl, combine the garlic powder, paprika, salt, and pepper.
3. In a separate bowl, pour the flour.
4. Place the catfish fillets into the bowl with the flour and toss until they are fully coated.
5. Heat a skillet over medium-high heat and add the olive oil and butter.
6. Once the butter is fully melted, add the floured catfish fillets. Cook for 5 minutes on each side until golden brown.
7. Transfer the cooked catfish fillets to a baking sheet and place in the preheated oven for 10 minutes.
8. Remove from oven and serve.

Nutrition information:
Serving size: 4 portions
Calories: 412
Total Fat: 16.6 g
Carbohydrates: 39.9 g
Protein: 27.7 g
Cholesterol: 47 mg
Sodium: 457 mg

88. Peanut Butter Fudge

This classic, delicious dessert recipe is the perfect way to satisfy your sweet tooth! Peanut Butter Fudge is a creamy, rich, and delectable treat that everyone will love.
Serving: 12 servings
Preparation Time: 20 minutes
Ready Time: 1 hour

Ingredients:
- 2 cups white sugar
- ½ cup butter
- 1 cup evaporated milk
- 1 cup peanut butter
- 2 teaspoons vanilla extract

- 3 cups mini marshmallows
- 2 cups semi-sweet chocolate chips

Instructions:
1. Grease a 9x13 inch baking pan with butter.
2. In a medium saucepan, combine the sugar, butter, and evaporated milk. Bring to a boil, stirring constantly, and cook for 2 minutes.
3. Remove from heat and add the peanut butter, vanilla extract, marshmallows, and chocolate chips. Stir until the marshmallows and chocolate chips are melted.
4. Pour the mixture into the greased baking pan.
5. Refrigerate for 1 hour until it sets.
6. Cut into 12 bars and enjoy!

Nutrition information: For one serving, Peanut Butter Fudge contains around 270 calories, 13g fat, 35g carbohydrates, and 4g protein.

89. Sweet Potato Waffles

Sweet Potato Waffles is a perfect brunch recipe that is tasty and offers a great way to get additional nutrients into your diet. It is versatile, vegan friendly and easy to make.
Serving: Serves 2
Preparation time: 15 minutes
Ready time: 25 minutes

Ingredients:
- 1 cup cooked sweet potato
- 1 cup plain flour
- 2 tablespoons maple syrup
- 1/2 teaspoon baking powder
- 1/2 teaspoon ground cinnamon
- 1 teaspoon ground nutmeg
- 2 tablespoons melted coconut oil or vegetable oil
- 1/2 cup almond milk

Instructions:

1. Preheat a waffle maker.
2. Mash the sweet potato and put it in a bowl.
3. Add the flour, maple syrup, baking powder, cinnamon, and nutmeg.
4. Mix until combined.
5. In a small bowl, combine the melted oil with the almond milk.
6. Slowly add the wet Ingredients to the dry Ingredients and mix until just combined.
7. Grease the waffle maker with a bit of oil and add a 1/3 cup of batter per waffle.
8. Cook for 4-5 minutes until golden brown and cooked through.
9. Serve with your favorite toppings.

Nutrition information: Each waffle provides approximately 200 calories, 22g of carbohydrates, 4g of fat, 5g of protein, 1g of fiber, and 20g of sugar.

90. Bourbon Balls

Bourbon Balls are a classic Southern confection, packed with flavor and easy to make. They're a combination of chocolate, nuts, and the sweetness of bourbon in a bite-sized form.
Serving: Makes 3 dozen
Preparation Time: 15 minutes
Ready Time: 1 hour 20 minutes

Ingredients:
- 1/4 cup bourbon
- 3/4 cup light corn syrup
- 3 tablespoons butter, melted
- 3 cups confectioners' sugar
- 2 tablespoons cocoa powder
- 2 cups finely chopped pecans
- 1/2 cup toasted coconut

Instructions:
1. In a large bowl, combine the bourbon, corn syrup, and butter.
2. In a separate bowl, mix together the confectioners' sugar and cocoa powder.

3. Gradually add the sugar and cocoa mixture to the wet Ingredients and stir until it forms a dough.
4. Add the chopped pecans and toasted coconut and stir to combine.
5. Roll the mixture into 1-inch balls and place on a parchment-lined baking sheet.
6. Place in the refrigerator for at least 1 hour before serving.

Nutrition information: Each serving (1 ball) contains: Calories: 83, Total Fat: 3.7 g, Sodium: 6 mg, Total Carbohydrate: 11 g, Protein: 1 g.

91. S'mores Pie

Indulge in the classic campfire treat with a twist with this delicious S'mores Pie! This no-bake dessert is packed with graham crackers, chocolate, marshmallows, and maraschino cherries.
Serving: 8
Preparation Time: 15 minutes
Ready Time: 2 hours

Ingredients:
- 2 cups graham cracker crumbs
- 1/2 cup butter, melted
- 1/4 cup granulated sugar
- 1 can sweetened condensed milk (14 oz)
- 1/2 cup semi-sweet or bittersweet chocolate chips
- 1/2 cup marshmallows
- 1/3 cup maraschino cherries, chopped

Instructions:
1. Preheat oven to 350°F and grease a 9-inch pie plate.
2. In a medium bowl, mix together the graham cracker crumbs, melted butter, and sugar. Press the mixture firmly and evenly into the bottom and up the sides of the prepared pie plate.
3. Bake for 10 minutes, then remove from oven and let cool for 10 minutes.
4. Pour the condensed milk evenly over the crust. Sprinkle the chocolate chips, marshmallows, and chopped cherries over the top.

5. Bake for 10 minutes, or until the marshmallows begin to brown.
6. Let cool before serving.

Nutrition information (per Serving):
- Calories: 400
- Total Fat: 19 g
- Saturated Fat: 11 g
- Sodium: 135 mg
- Carbohydrates: 51 g
- Fiber: 1.3 g
- Protein: 5 g

92. Shrimp and Grits

Shrimp and Grits is a classic Southern dish that is made with plump shrimp, creamy cheesy grits, and a flavorful tomato-based sauce.
Serving: Serves 4.
Preparation time: 10 minutes.
Ready time: 25 minutes.

Ingredients:
- 1/2 cup onion, diced
- 1 tablespoon garlic, minced
- 2 tablespoons butter
- 8 ounces cooked and peeled shrimp
- 1/2 cup roasted red peppers, diced
- 1/4 cup white wine
- 1/4 teaspoon black pepper
- 2 cups quick-cooking grits
- 4 ounces cheddar cheese, shredded
- 2 tablespoons chopped parsley

Instructions:
1. Heat the butter in a large skillet over medium-high heat. Add the onion and garlic and cook until the onion is softened and lightly browned, about 5 minutes.

2. Add the shrimp and red peppers and cook for 2 minutes. Add the white wine and season with black pepper.
3. Reduce the heat to low and simmer until most of the liquid has evaporated, about 5 minutes.
4. Meanwhile, cook the grits according to the package directions.
5. When the grits are done cooking, stir in the cheese until melted.
6. Divide the grits among four serving bowls and top with the shrimp mixture. Sprinkle with parsley and serve.

Nutrition information: 189 calories, 8.9 g fat, 20.3 g carbohydrates, 11.5 g protein per serving.

93. Cherry Cobbler

Cherry cobbler is a classic American dessert made with fresh cherries, a buttery biscuit topping, and just a hint of cinnamon. It's a simple and delicious summer treat.
Serving: 6-8
Preparation time: 10 minutes
Ready time: 45 minutes

Ingredients:
- 4 cups fresh or frozen cherries, pitted
- 2/3 cup granulated sugar
- 2 tablespoons cornstarch
- 2 tablespoons fresh lemon juice
- 1 teaspoon ground cinnamon
- 1/4 teaspoon salt
- 2/3 cup all-purpose flour
- 2 tablespoons granulated sugar
- 4 tablespoons cold butter, cut into small cubes
- 2 teaspoons baking powder
- 1/4 teaspoon baking soda
- 1/4 cup milk

Instructions:
1. Preheat oven to 375°F. Grease an 8-by-8-inch baking dish.

2. In a medium bowl, mix the cherries, 2/3 cup sugar, cornstarch, lemon juice, cinnamon, and salt. Add the mixture to the prepared baking dish.
3. In a medium bowl, whisk together the flour, 2 tablespoons sugar, baking powder, and baking soda. Cut the butter into the flour mixture until it resembles coarse crumbs. Add the milk and mix until a soft dough forms.
4. Drop dollops of the dough over the cherry mixture.
5. Bake for 35 to 40 minutes or until the cherries are bubbly and the topping is golden brown. Serve warm.

Nutrition information:
Calories: 243, Fat: 8g, Carbohydrates: 44g, Protein: 2g, Sodium: 211mg, Fiber: 2g

94. Caramel Apple Bread

Caramel Apple Bread is a delicious and sweet bread that combines the flavors of apples and caramel into one. It is a perfect snack to enjoy and can be served as a dessert.
Serving: Serves 8
Preparation Time: 20 minutes
Ready Time: 1 hour, 10 minutes

Ingredients:
- 2 cups all-purpose flour
- 2 teaspoons baking powder
- 1/4 teaspoon baking soda
- 1/4 teaspoon salt
- 2 teaspoons ground cinnamon
- 3/4 cup white sugar
- 1/2 cup butter, melted
- 2 eggs, lightly beaten
- 2 teaspoons vanilla extract
- 1 cup chopped apples
- 1/2 cup chopped pecans
- 1/2 cup caramel sauce

Instructions:

1. Preheat oven to 350 degrees F (175 degrees C). Grease a 9x5 inch loaf pan.
2. In a medium bowl, whisk together the flour, baking powder, baking soda, salt, and cinnamon.
3. In a separate bowl, cream together the sugar and butter. Beat in the eggs one at a time, then stir in the vanilla.
4. Gradually beat in the flour mixture, stirring just until blended.
5. Fold in the apples and pecans.
6. Pour half the batter into the prepared pan. Drizzle with half the caramel sauce. Top with the remaining batter, and drizzle with the remaining caramel.
7. Bake for 55 to 65 minutes, or until a toothpick inserted into the center of the bread comes out clean. Cool in the pan for 10 minutes, then turn out onto a cooling rack.

Nutrition information:
Calories: 341 kcal; Total Fat: 15.6g; Saturated Fat: 7.8g; Cholesterol: 69mg; Sodium: 246mg; Total Carbohydrates: 43.1g; Dietary Fiber: 1.7g; Sugars: 22.7g; Protein: 5g

95. Buttermilk Ranch Biscuits

Buttermilk Ranch Biscuits are fluffy and delicious homemade biscuits flavored with ranch seasoning that will become a family favorite!
Serving: 12
Preparation Time: 10 minutes
Ready Time: 20 minutes

Ingredients:
2 cups All-Purpose Flour
1 teaspoon Baking Powder
1 teaspoon Baking Soda
3/4 teaspoon Salt
3 tablespoons Cold Unsalted Butter
1 cup buttermilk
1/4 cup Sour Cream
2 Tablespoons Ranch Seasoning

Instructions:
1. Preheat oven to 425 degrees Fahrenheit and line a baking sheet with parchment paper or a silicone baking mat.
2. In a medium bowl, whisk together flour, baking powder, baking soda, and salt.
3. Cut the butter into small cubes and add to the flour mixture. Using a pastry cutter or two forks, cut the butter into the flour mixture until it resembles coarse crumbs.
4. Create a well in the center of the flour mixture and pour in the buttermilk, sour cream, and ranch seasoning. Stir until just combined.
5. Turn the dough out onto a lightly floured surface and knead the dough about 5 times.
6. Using a rolling pin, roll the dough into a 1" thick circle. Cut out 12 even rounds using a biscuit cutter or a drinking glass. Place the biscuits on the prepared baking sheet.
7. Bake for 15-20 minutes or until the edges are golden brown.

Nutrition information:
Serving Size: 1 Biscuit
Calories: 165
Total Fat: 6g
Total Carbohydrates: 24g
Protein: 3g
Sugar: 2g
Cholesterol: 8mg
Sodium: 264mg

96. Bourbon-Soaked Cherry Cake

Give your classic cherry cake a bit of a twist by soaking the cherries in bourbon before baking. This bourbon-soaked cherry cake is truly a pleasure to behold and to consume.
Serving: 8-10
Preparation time: 15 minutes
Ready time: 1 hour 25 minutes

Ingredients:
- 2 cups cherries, pitted and halved

- 1/2 cup bourbon
- 2 1/2 cups all-purpose flour
- 1 teaspoon baking powder
- 1 teaspoon baking soda
- 1 teaspoon salt
- 3/4 cup butter
- 1/2 cup shortening
- 2 cups granulated sugar
- 4 eggs
- 1 teaspoon almond extract
- 1 teaspoon vanilla extract

Instructions:
1. In a bowl, combine the cherries and bourbon and let sit for 10 minutes, stirring occasionally.
2. Preheat the oven to 350°F.
3. In a separate bowl, combine the flour, baking powder, baking soda, and salt.
4. In a large bowl, cream together the butter, shortening, and sugar until light and fluffy. Add the eggs one at a time, beating well after each addition.
5. Gradually add the dry Ingredients to the butter mixture, mixing well.
6. Drain the cherries, and fold them into the batter. Stir in the almond and vanilla extracts.
7. Pour the batter into a greased and floured 9x13 inch pan and bake for 1 hour 15 minutes to 1 hour 25 minutes, or until a toothpick inserted into the center comes out clean.

Nutrition information: Serving size: 1 slice, Calories: 350, Total Fat: 16g, Cholesterol: 55mg, Sodium: 410mg, Carbohydrates: 46g, Sugar: 28g, Protein: 4g.

97. Southern Fried Apples

Southern Fried Apples are a comfort-food classic, beloved by southerners of all ages. This recipe is simple and delicious—perfect for dessert or as an accompaniment to a hearty entrée.
Serving: 2-4

Preparation Time: 15 minutes
Ready Time: 40 minutes

Ingredients:
- 4 Granny Smith apples
- 1/2 cup sugar
- 1/2 cup + 2 tbs all-purpose flour
- ½ teaspoon of ground cinnamon
- ½ teaspoon of freshly-ground nutmeg
- 3/4 teaspoon of freshly-ground cardamom
- 1/2 cup butter, melted
- 1/4 cup water

Instructions:
1. Preheat oven to 350°F.
2. Peel and core apples, then cut into wedges.
3. In a shallow bowl, mix together the sugar, flour, cinnamon, nutmeg, and cardamom.
4. Dip the apple wedges in the sugar-flour mixture and coat evenly.
5. Place the apples in an 8-inch baking dish.
6. In a small bowl, mix together the melted butter and water.
7. Pour the butter-water mixture over the apples.
8. Bake at 350°F for 40 minutes, stirring occasionally.

Nutrition information:
Calories: 302, Totalfat: 8 grams, Saturated fat: 5grams, Cholesterol: 20 milligrams, Sodium: 99 milligrams, Carbohydrates: 55 grams, Dietary fiber: 3 grams, Protein: 3 grams.

98. Mississippi Mud Cookies

Mississippi Mud Cookies are a delicious treat that is perfect for any occasion. This recipe combines ooey-gooey marshmallows, chocolate and graham crackers for a delightful cookie that is sure to be a hit.
Serving: Makes about 36 cookies
Preparation Time: 30 minutes
Ready Time: 2 hours

Ingredients:

- ½ cup (113 g) butter, melted
- 2 cups (468 g) brown sugar
- 2 teaspoons (10 ml) vanilla extract
- 2 eggs, beaten
- 2 ¾ cups (343 g) all-purpose flour
- 2/3 cup (94 g) cocoa powder
- 1 teaspoon (5 g) baking soda
- ¼ teaspoon (2 g) salt
- 1 cup (140 g) miniature marshmallows
- 2 cups (255 g) graham cracker crumbs
- 10 ounces (284 g) semi-sweet chocolate chips

Instructions:

1. Preheat oven to 350°F (177°C).
2. In a large bowl, cream together butter, sugar, vanilla and eggs.
3. In a separate bowl whisk together flour, cocoa powder, baking soda and salt.
4. Gradually add the dry Ingredients to the wet Ingredients and mix until well combined.
5. Fold in miniature marshmallows, graham cracker crumbs and chocolate chips.
6. Drop heaping tablespoons of dough onto a parchment lined baking sheet.
7. Bake for 8-10 minutes.

Nutrition information (per cookie):

Calories – 182 kcal, Fat – 7g, Carbohydrates – 27g, Protein – 2g, Fiber – 1g

CONCLUSION

As we've seen, Bite into the South: 98 Paula Deen's Baking Delights is the perfect cookbook for anyone looking to explore the flavor and culture of the South. The recipes included in the book provide an accessible and delicious way to get a taste of South, with a wide range of regional specialties like biscuits and gravy, peach cobbler, and sweet tea. The cookbook also includes detailed guides to help you get the most out of your baking experience, from step-by-step instructions to tips to avoid common mistakes.

Overall, Bite into the South: 98 Paula Deen's Baking Delights is a great choice for anyone looking to explore regional cuisine. With its delicious recipes and helpful guides, this cookbook is sure to be a hit with anyone interested in the flavors of the South. The recipes can be tailored to fit any gathering, from intimate dinner parties to large gatherings of friends and family. Plus, with over 90 recipes in the book, you can explore a wide range of classic regional dishes and experiment with various baking techniques.

Cooking traditional dishes from the South is a great way to experience the flavors of the region and to connect with its people and culture. Bite into the South: 98 Paula Deen's Baking Delights provides an excellent place to start. From the detailed instruction guides to the flavorful recipes, this book offers a wonderful way to explore and enjoy the cuisine of the South. So, if you've been looking for a way to truly bite into the South, this cookbook is a great choice!